FAITH THAT GOES FURTHER

DAYTON

FAITH THAT GOES FURTHER

FACING THE
CONTRADICTIONS
OF LIFE

MULTNOMAH PRESS
PORTLAND, OREGON 97266

Other books by Edward R. Dayton:
   Whatever Happened to Commitment?
   The Christian Leader's Sixty Second Management Guide
   That Everyone May Hear
   Planning Strategies for World Evangelization
   God's Purpose/Man's Plans
   The Christian Executive
   Strategy for Living
   Strategy for Christian Leadership
   The Art of Management for Christian Leaders

Unless otherwise indentified, scripture references in this volume are from J. B. Phillips: The New Testament in Modern English, revised edition. © J. B. Phillips 1958, 1960, 1972. Used by permission of Macmillan Publishing Co., Inc.

Verses marked NIV are from the Holy Bible: New International Version, copyright 1978 by the New York International Bible Society. Used by permission of Zondervan Bible Publishers.

Verses marked RSV are from the Revised Standard Version of the Bible, copyright 1946, 1952, © 1971, 1973, Division of Christian Education, National Council of the Churches of Christ in the USA.

Verses marked TLB are taken from The Living Bible, copyright 1971 by Tyndale House Publishers, Wheaton, Ill.

Verses marked TEV are from the Good News Bible; copyright © American Bible Society 1976.

Cover design by Larry Ulmer

FAITH THAT GOES FURTHER
© 1984 by Multnomah Press
Portland, Oregon 97266

Printed in the United States of America

84 85 86 87 88 89 90 – 10 9 8 7 6 5 4 3 2 1

For all who once were *Pathfinders*.
And for those who would like to be.

CONTENTS

FOREWORD

Ed Dayton and I first met at the Berlin Congress on Evangelism in 1966. We were literally "behind the scenes" where he was working on a display and I was autographing some books.

It was a fitting beginning of our friendship. Both Ed and I have been actively involved in world evangelism, he with the ministries of World Vision, I as an evangelist with Billy Graham. But we have both also been active "behind the scenes" in the strategy of world evangelization, particularly as we have worked together on the Lausanne Committee for World Evangelization.

So it strikes me that Ed's new study of James takes us "behind the scenes," so to speak, into the life of a Christian activist. James is a very practical epistle which shows how Christian faith translates into action. But that translation is not always easy. To be a Christian does not mean that we will always have easy answers; sometimes it raises harder questions. What does it mean to have "the faith of our Lord Jesus Christ" lived out in terms of our language, our lifestyle, our attitudes, our daily schedules, our long-range planning, our troubles and sicknesses and joys?

I have a friend who says she has never had any difficulty in believing, that from childhood hers has been a simple faith. I know that's true in terms of her belief. But as I have observed her coping with the demands of being a wife, a mother, and a church leader, I have also seen her many times puzzled by the perplexities of living out her faith.

Here is where *Faith That Goes Further* is helpful. Ed Dayton has given us not a commentary, but rather "musings," thoughts on God's inspired Word in James as it bears on the complexities of his life. By happy coincidence, I received Ed's manuscript just as my wife Jeannie had finished several months of teaching James to her weekly Bible class and just as I was ending a personal devotional study of this epistle. My own study was interwoven with some decisions I had to make. As a result, we found Ed's book intensely interesting.

FOREWORD

Ed Dayton is known to many as writer, strategist, speaker, executive. But here, "behind the scenes" of his busy life, he shows how the steady light of God's sure, heavenly Word brings direction to our sometimes confusing earthly discipleship.

I thank God for His gift of Ed to the church. I thank Ed for the gift of this book to all of us.

Leighton Ford

INTRODUCTION

This is a book about Christian maturity, a maturity lived in paradox. It is a book written for Christians, those who name Jesus as God. In many ways it is a call to a deeper faith, a larger trust. It is not a book of answers, of formulas, or of keys to success. I've tried to go deeper than that, for answers or formulas only last for a while. It is the questions that are eternal.

The Road I Have Traveled

The road that I have traveled so far has been pitted and rough at times. There have been days when the valleys seemed impossibly deep and the rivers too wide to cross. But through it all there has been a returning sense of God's presence and a feeling of growing— not my growth alone, but His within me.

It has been an exciting life. If I had to do it over again, I would change very little. As a family we have lived East, West, and in the middle. Three daughters are married. An eighteen-year-old son keeps me alert and young at the same time. I have been an engineer, an aerospace manager, a mission executive. When I reached the age of forty, we started a new life and went to seminary.

Sixteen years ago I joined World Vision as director of a division called MARC (Missions Advanced Research and Communication Center). The task has taken me all over the world. I've experienced the hopelessness of an India ghetto and the exhilaration of dynamic churches in Brazil. I have smelled the stench of war and sat under a billion stars in Northern Kenya while marveling at the wonder of God's creation.

But I suspect that I have learned the most from the everyday business of teaching a Bible class of about seventy-five couples in their mid-thirties. We called ourselves "Pathfinders." We were much like a congregation within the congregation of our large church, Lake Avenue Congregational, in Pasadena.

For me, teaching has to be existential—to have reality, results, if you will. And so I have wept with my Pathfinder friends, prayed for them and with them; I have been blessed by them and sometimes hurt. I have watched them wrestle back and forth with the pull of a middle-class American culture that calls out to them to "Grab all the gusto you can get!" and with the inner urging of that still small voice that quietly claims that the meek shall inherit the earth. At times they have made me angry, not so much with them as with my own inability to help them *see* (and many times my failure to learn what they had to teach me).

But they grew. We were growing together, I believe. Sometimes God had used another seminar, another how-to-do-it book. (I've written some of those, too!) But mostly we learned to trust God *for answers that weren't there.* Why did Palmer have to die so young? Why had young Jamie been in the hospital over ninety times? Why did Bob have M.S.? Why did Wayne break his leg in a fall? Why are some doing so well financially while others hardly make it? Why have some of the missionaries who have gone out from our class had such difficult times? I don't know.

I don't know *intellectually.* But in the midst of all these things we slowly learned that above all God wants us to trust Him—not blindly, not without taking thought, but with our eyes wide open and our minds in gear.

I say "we." My wife Marge has been a fellow traveler on this spiritual journey. I went to seminary at forty. She started back to school at forty-five and got her master's in theology at fifty-two. Her gifts are in counseling, and she has been a licensed marriage and family counselor during these years. In learning more about herself she has helped me understand myself better. Even though I'm not too sure what that means. Does one ever really know oneself? What a paradox I find myself to be.

Paradox—Apparent Contradictions

Paradox, tension, . . . and faith. To me those are dimensions of the Christian life. To accept the paradox, those apparent contradictions, is to live in the tension of a kingdom come and yet to arrive; that is what faith is all about. To refuse to accept the paradox is to play God. To refuse to accept the Christian life as a struggle, a tension, is to deny the Bible. To reject faith is to reject Christ. What we need is a faith that goes further.

This book is part of a journey. I use the word journey purposely. I am sure that mine are not the final answers; it's not certain I have even all the right questions. I'm sure I have much more to learn. I'm much more certain about the things I affirm than the things I deny.

I have used the book of James as a road map, but there are side journeys, too. Paul and Peter have their say.

Before we begin, let me make two comments about God's Word. First, Scripture should always be viewed as a whole. It is fine to compare Scripture with Scripture, but the first paradox we face is that Scripture is human even while it is divine, God-breathed. The book of James is a letter from the Lord's brother James to a group of people. We need to encounter it as a whole so that what we say, and what we conclude, comes out from the text and does not start with us. Consequently, I have reproduced James's entire letter.

Second, words must always be seen in context. Words mean different things in different settings. Take the word *bar*. As a noun it has at least seven general meanings. When I tell you something is a bar, you have no way of telling what I mean until I say more. If I say that I was standing at the bar, you know that I do not mean a musical notation or a lace or embroidery. If I tell you I was in a courtroom, you know I was not standing at a food counter and am probably in the prisoner's dock. To compare the various meanings of the word bar is therefore only useful when we look at the meanings given by the context.

I have chosen to use J. B. Phillips's "paraphrase" primarily to give a fresh look at what may be some well-read and well-remembered words. Because I am much more familiar with other translations, I have used these, too. Every now and then, in an attempt to throw more light on the passage, light that perhaps we need to clearly see our way, I have turned aside from the journey and centered on other parts of God's Word.

Two men had a great deal to do with keeping me on course and encouraging me. My beloved colleague Paul Rees was merciless in his reading of an earlier manuscript, as only a real friend can be. David Fraser, another well-loved fellow worker, kept reading and nudging me on. I am grateful.

Ed Dayton

1
BEGINNINGS

Have you ever tried to picture what it's like to die and be reborn? I don't mean just spiritually, but physically. To be dead, buried, and raised?

Imagine a scene from a movie about the American Civil War. In the opening scene we move inside a crowded military prison. The prisoners are languishing, despairing of ever being free. They have been here too long. It seems the war will never end. The day-to-day monotony of the cells is unrelieved. High walls loom around the small open yard, walls stared at so long that each prisoner can close his eyes and remember each detail. Many are sick, some more from boredom than disease.

Will anyone ever escape? Will the war that has placed them here ever be over? Over in that corner one of the prisoners is dying of pneumonia. We know nothing about him, except that his hands grasp a well-worn Bible. As we watch, a disinterested doctor pronounces him dead. His body is placed in a crude pine coffin and loaded onto a flat wagon pulled by two horses. The creaking wagon proceeds slowly through the high wooden gate and makes its way to a burial ground atop a rolling hill about a half mile away. An oblong hole is dug. The pine box is lowered into the ground and quickly covered. A crude wooden marker is placed on the mound of dirt. The burial party with its team of horses leaves, and all is quiet.

Do you not know that all of us who have been baptized into Christ Jesus were baptized into his death? We were

15

> buried therefore with him by baptism into death, so that as Christ was raised from the dead by the glory of the Father, we too might walk in newness of life (Romans 6:3, 4 RSV).

Buried. The Christian is buried with Christ. But a new day dawns and with it a new life. This soldier who had died rises to a new life. The bonds of death are broken. The coffin is shattered. A new man comes forth. He stands upon the hill and surveys the world around him. A gentle breeze is blowing. The field flowers have a brightness and intensity that he never knew before. Beautiful. The sky is blue, a blue unlike any earthly blue. And all around as far as the eye can see, the earth is fresh and lovely. He breathes deeply, sensing how *different* everything has become, and with enthusiasm and exultation moves out to a new life in Christ.

We understand now that this movie is a metaphor. Instead of ascending to heaven, this man is to live a new life on earth. What will it be like?

> I through the law died to the law, that I might live to God. . . . the life I now live in the flesh I live by faith in the son of God, who loved me and gave himself for me (Galatians 2:19, 20 RSV).

We see the man again, bewildered. Where to go? What road to take? There seem to be no road signs, no landmarks. But who is that walking over there? That man seems to have found a path in the field. Perhaps he knows the road. The camera follows as the two greet each other.

As a Christian starts his new journey, he often finds others who believe that they have found (at that moment) just the right path. "Take this road." "Go that way." "Study this course." "Join this local fellowship." Roadways take shape. Signposts appear. The flowers of the fields of freedom are exchanged for the hustle of a city of laws. Answers are given and accepted. Rules are formed, liturgies written. What was once a simple trust is now exchanged for all too pat answers. And slowly, almost imperceptibly at first, the walls of that prison seem to grow back. What started out as a marvelous new journey becomes almost as dull a routine as life in the prison.

A Life of Formulas—Not Flowers

I've watched it happen. I've seen a dynamic faith of a born-again believer slowly become static and lifeless, simply a series of propositions to be discussed and defended. Faith becomes something out there, other worldly. And as faith becomes abstract, so does the Christian life. Oh, the form is there. But what of life? What of that feeling of newness? Where have all the flowers gone?

The writer to the Hebrews calls us to "leave behind the elementary teaching about Christ and go forward to adult understanding. Let us not lay over and over again the foundation truths—repentance from the deeds which led to death, believing in God, the teaching of baptism and laying-on of hands, belief in the resurrection of the dead and the final judgment. No, if God allows, let us go on" (Hebrews 6:1-3).

Let us go on!

The mature Christian is one who has tested God's Word and found that it *works*. His or hers is not a maturity based just on ideas. It is the maturity of experience, of testing, of living. It is a life based not so much on a set of rules as on a trust in God's love and grace and Holy Spirit.

We live in a day when people are seeking rules. And no wonder! There are so many voices calling to us. Life seems to become more complicated every day. Too many new people. Too many interpersonal intersections. How much more comfortable it is to have someone else tell us how to live than to live "in Christ."

Formulas are so handy. The trouble is that the instructions given so easily are seldom universal. They don't always apply. They are temporal, bound by time. For Christians are always growing or decaying. The Bible has no picture of a Christian standing still. In the flush of a new-found faith, a new hope, a Savior who can keep, and a God who is interested in us as individuals, we perhaps imagine that we are embarking on a grand adventure in which our certitude will increase every day. We expect that each day as we "grow in Christ" we will have more and more (very specific) answers to life's deepest questions. We will have a better understanding of how the world "works."

More Questions, Fewer Answers

But as we dig deeper into God's Word, and as we allow the Holy Spirit to dig deeper into our own lives, we discover that those things which we hoped were going to be very straightforward at times become very difficult. And as the Bible sensitizes us to the kind of a world God intends, the questions multiply. Why is it, for example, that some of the best people we know, those with a moral standard far higher than ours, turn away from the Savior whom we love?

Why, we ask with the psalmist, do the ungodly prosper?

The answers do not come easily. Sometimes they never come at all. But to some they come too quickly. A Bible verse is accepted and memorized as an "answer." "Train up a child in the way he should go and when he is old he will not depart from the way thereof," we quote, never stopping to ask the next question, "How do I know the way?"

Christian growth is painful—but profitable. As we grow we discover that we don't *have* to have a pat answer for every situation. Most of the time there are no universal, standard answers. Experience tells us things don't always add up the way we would like them to. And the Bible confirms our experience.

The philosophers of this world continually seek to close the circle of the meaning of life. They want data and formulas they can control. They seek to understand, to know, to put the world together in some explainable way. Behind their seeking is the assumption that one can know, one can explain.[1]

The Christian can fall into the same trap.[2] But the circle of human understanding refuses to close. We come at it from one side, say God's sovereignty, and we keep working our way around until we are faced with the apparent fact of human freedom. Both ideas don't fit! And slowly, too slowly, we learn that what appears to the world as foolish contradictions are in fact God's good way for us. Faith and works do go together. God's sovereignty and our freedom do work out!

When Contradictions Make Divine Sense

It is the thesis of this book that the Bible is full of apparent contradictions—paradoxes—both stated and implied. I believe that we have spent so much time and energy trying to defend the Bible against science-so-called that we have fallen into the trap of believing that "truth" and "fact" are the same thing. Such ideas force us to search for formulas. Two plus two must equal four, mustn't it? We instinctively turn away from paradox. But our formulas just don't work when we try to solve the riddle of God's control of all things and our freedom, or Christ's divinity and Jesus' humanness.

We need to move beyond such a search for formulas and commit ourselves to accept God's revelation of His system. He who loses his life shall find it!

The life that is Christian is a continual search for middle ground in the midst of paradox.[3] *The mark of the mature Christian is an ability to ac-*

cept the paradox of God's Word and to live a life in light of that paradox; to hold the extremes of what we understand and what we can't understand in tension, and to see them bonded together by the mystery of faith.

In a Western culture which is ever more complicated, ever more difficult to understand, ever bombarding us with seemingly new questions, we can find that calm assurance that all things do work together for good. If God is the One who is *for* us, then in the midst of all of the pressures of everyday living there is that peaceful center where faith reigns and paradox becomes unimportant.[4]

Notes

1. Peter Berger and others give us some good insight into the openendedness of the American view of life. In *The Homeless Mind*, they point out that Westerners have come to view life as unfinished with improvement always possible. This in turn has led to a continuous searching inward. "How can I do better? How can I *be* better?" The result is a growing dissatisfaction with ourselves and a growing alienation from others. See also Lasch, *The Culture of Narcissism*.

2. What few of us realize is how we are influenced by our Western technological culture that assumes, "There is an answer for everything. Every part has its interchangeable replacement." I have discussed the impact of American culture on American Christianity at length in *Whatever Happened to Commitment?*

3. Virginia Mollenkott has expressed it in another way in the title of her book, *In Search of Balance*.

4. Nels Ferré calls it *The Extreme Center*.

2
YOUR BROTHER IS YOUR LORD

James, a servant of God and of the Lord Jesus Christ,
sends greeting to the twelve dispersed tribes (James 1:1).

Modern scholarship points to James, the Lord's brother, as the
author of this letter bearing his name. James was Jesus' physical half
brother. He was the ruling elder of the church at Jerusalem and the
"pillar of the church." Certainly no one could be closer than a
brother. Jesus loved him so much that, after His resurrection, He ap-
peared to James before His other remaining disciples (1 Corinthians
15:7).

Not only was James close to Jesus, but he rose to a position of
leadership in the mother church at Jerusalem. We tend to think of
Peter as head of the church, but when Peter was released miracu-
lously from prison, he told his friends to "Tell this to James . . ."
(Acts 12:17). History tells that James was thought of as one of the
most saintly men in Jerusalem.[1] We see him again leading the con-
ference in Jerusalem in Acts 15.

But when this leader of the church refers to his fleshly brother,
how does he refer to himself and how does he refer to Jesus? First,
he calls himself a slave or bondservant. A slave of Rome was in complete subjection to a master. James sees himself stripped of any of
the prerogatives of birth, a person with no rights, no privileges.
What an attitude! How often I find myself demanding my rights.
"But that's not fair, Lord," I complain. "After all, if I am your

brother, things like this shouldn't happen to me!"

Second, he addresses Jesus as "Lord," the One who created the universe and upholds it by His power. One would think that James of all people would consider himself on a more equal footing with Jesus. How does "Lord" fit with "brother"?

Bondservant and *Lord*. Do we really understand what that means? Turn to Colossians 1:15-18.[2]

> Now Christ is the visible expression of the invisible God. He was born before creation began, for it was through him that everything was made, whether heavenly or earthly, seen or unseen. Through him, and for him, also, were created power and dominion, ownership and authority. In fact, all things were created through, and for, him. He is both the first principle and the upholding principle of the whole scheme of creation. And now he is the head of the Body which is the Church. He is the Beginning, the first to be born from the dead, which gives him pre-eminence over all things (Colossians 1:15-18).

James also calls Him "Christ," the Greek word for Messiah, the anointed One, the promised Savior of Israel. He calls Him the "Lord of Glory" (James 2:1, RSV).

Jesus: Brother or Friend or . . . Lord?

How are we to think of such a Lord Jesus Christ? Do we misread the Bible when we sing "What a friend we have in Jesus"? Is Jesus so far beyond us that He is not to be touched?

Paul tells us in his letter to the Romans that we are children of God and brothers of Christ (Romans 8:14, 17a, 29). And so we are. We are like Abraham, who James tells us "believed God, and it was reckoned unto him for righteousness; and he was called the friend of God" (James 2:23).

But if we see Jesus only as the one who sticks closer than a brother, the dear Friend who is always there, we will miss the fact that this is a relationship with *God Himself*.

On the other hand, if we are so awed by the majesty of the Lord that we never come to rely on Him as a *person* who suffered all we have suffered, we will miss the fellowship He so graciously offers.

Jesus is a man. Jesus is God. How does that fit together? From our viewpoint it's a paradox. How do we find a balance? Brother-to-brother or servant-to-Lord? Both! But never just one. We need to live and relate to Him in the midst of this tension.

Have you become so familiar with Jesus that you have forgotten that the very universe is held together by His word? Has He perhaps been so internalized in your thoughts, become such an abstract idea, that He is no longer a person? Fall down and worship Him! Stand with the psalmist and declare the wonder of it all. "The heavens declare the glory of God, and the firmament shows His handiwork" (Psalm 19:1, KJV).

Have you stood so in awe of the Son of God that He is just a distant figure of history? "And so, dear brothers, now we may walk right into the very Holy of Holies where God is, because of the blood of Jesus" (Hebrews 10:19, TLB).

Reach up and take His hand. It's always there.

Notes

1. James was such a man of prayer, legend tells us his knees were calloused from kneeling upon them.

2. There is an even deeper paradox here, the paradox of Jesus as truly man and truly God. This paradox is so deep that, through the ages, the church has only been able to affirm it, never explain it. The closest anyone has come is at the Council of Nicea in 325 A.D. which could only affirm, as does our Nicene Creed, that Jesus and the Father are of the same substance, even while at the same time Jesus is man.

3
WELCOME TRIALS
WITH JOY

When all kinds of trials and temptations crowd into your lives, my brothers, don't resent them as intruders, but welcome them as friends! Realise that they come to test your faith and to produce in you the quality of endurance. But let the process go on until that endurance is fully developed, and you will find you have become men of mature character, men of integrity with no weak spots (James 1:2-4).

The world seeks happiness; the Christian experiences joy.

While men and women of the world are seeking pleasure and fulfillment in themselves, the Christian knows that real happiness is found in a relationship. The Christian rests in the confidence of a God Who is for him or her: "In my opinion whatever we may have to go through now is less than nothing compared with the magnificent future God has in store for us" (Romans 8:18). *The magnificent future God has in store for us.* What a fantastic idea that is! "In face of all this, what is there left to say? If God is for us, who can be against us?" (Romans 8:31).

The world sees trials and temptations as things to avoid. Common sense tells us to stay away from trouble. James tells us, "When all kind of trials and temptations crowd into your lives, my brothers, don't resent them as intruders, but welcome them as friends!"

Our friend from the world responds, "Nonsense!" James counters, "Realise that they come to test your faith and to produce in you a quality of endurance." James does not claim that there is no pain, no painful tension. Neither does Paul: "And it is plain, too, that we who have a foretaste of the Spirit are in a state of painful tension, while we wait for that redemption of our bodies which will mean that we have realised our full sonship in him" (Romans 8:23).

But is a trial really something to be pleased with?

The RSV translates James 1:2, "Count it all joy, my brethren, when you meet various trials. . . ." Do joy and trials go together? Is it possible that there *is* a relationship between them?

Putting Joy and Trials Together

Let's examine the biblical idea of "joy." What is it? Jesus contrasts joy with sorrow (John 16:20). Joy is that which comes when sorrow disappears. But He goes on to state that the kind of joy that never departs will come when He comes. "So you have sorrow now, but I will see you again and your hearts will rejoice, and no one will take your joy from you" (John 16:22, RSV).

In the book of Acts, joy is a mark of the life of the early church. In Acts 13, after the disciples have been run out of town, we find them "filled with joy and with the Holy Spirit" (Acts 13:52, RSV). *Filled* with joy and the Holy Spirit. Joy has a quality that fills. It is a fruit of the Holy Spirit (Galatians 5:22), and it is therefore not something to be conjured up by being in the right setting or with the right people. It comes out of something, is the fruit of something. "Without having seen him you love him; though you do not now see him you believe in him and rejoice with unutterable and exalted joy" (1 Peter 1:8, RSV).

Joy is also a *response.* It has a quiet confidence that is based on experience. I see God at work: that is my experience. I rejoice: that is my response.

But why rejoice in the midst of trial, or if not in the midst of it, because trials have arrived? James looks at the trials of life as testings. And in the same way any test is designed to discover the quality of that which is being tested, so trials test the quality of our Christian life.

Rejoice in trials means rejoice in testings. Of course there are many different kinds of tests in life. The tests James speaks of are not so much ones of competition with others as tests of ourselves. They are tests of endurance.

Can you hang in there through the difficult and unpleasant task your boss may have given you? Can you take the hardships that come along and keep trusting God? Can you resist the temptation to sin that is always present? If you can, you will come out a stronger and more confident person and therefore one who can rejoice in what God is doing in your life.

If we look for one biblical example of testing it would be the case of Abraham. For reasons unknown to Abraham, God asked him to offer his only son as a sacrifice. When his faith was put to the test, Abraham's response was one of absolute trust. "Think of Abraham, our ancestor. Wasn't it his action which really justified him in God's sight when *his faith* led him to offer his son Isaac on the altar?" (James 2:21).

Does not all of our Christian life teach us the same lesson? It is not until we have been through the fire that we can face it with confidence. Sometimes testing develops confidence in ourselves or an assurance because of the gifts and abilities God has given us. At other times testing produces the confidence of knowing that God will lead us through without any help from our efforts.

When we are young we are afraid of the valley. As we see the path descending into the shadow, we cry out, "I'm afraid!" As we mature in Christ, we may be no less afraid, but another voice says, "You have walked this way before. It is all right. I am with you."

Does this mean that we become Stoics, holding in our emotions? Are we to push on, grim-faced and jaws set? No. We are not asked to put aside human emotion or to replace it with some *super*human emotion. "If one member suffers, all suffer together" (1 Corinthians 12:26, RSV). "Weep with those who weep" (Romans 12:15, RSV). We are asked to see that these trials and testings can be used by God to produce a stability that in turn can be put to godly use.

Some years ago, my niece was tragically killed on her seventeenth birthday. While I attended her funeral in Norman, Oklahoma, my sister showed me a suspicious lesion on her tongue. Two weeks later she underwent surgery at Mayo Clinic. The night before she was to be discharged from the hospital, she died of a hemorrhage. Within three weeks a family had been shattered. It hurt. I hurt.

At the time I was just starting a study of 2 Corinthians. Paul's words meant more to me than they ever had: "[God] comforts us in all our affliction, so that we may be able to comfort those who are in any affliction . . ." (2 Corinthians 1:4, RSV).

So I grew a little. And the next time I stood by the side of one who had lost a loved one, I was different. I sensed it, and the person I was with seemed to know it, too. Words weren't necessary. We find it a part of life that we have great difficulty in relating to those who are going through something that is completely outside our own experience. Having had a similar experience gives us a unique ability to make the right response. When you have experienced the death of a close friend or loved one, you understand what someone who is in the midst of that same experience needs the most: your presence and your assurance you have been through the same situation, and that it is "all right."

The World Is a Hurting Place

All the world experiences suffering. The Bible pictures the world as fallen. The primary cause of it all was man's rebellion and its result. "God gave them up," we read three times in the first chapter of Romans (1:24, 26, 28). The entire world is being strangled by the results of sin in its culture and in its subjection to the whims of a fallen natural world. We are not only buffeted by the desires of sinful men, but we are also continually subject to the physical elements of the world in which we find ourselves.[1] People sin against us and seek our harm. Earthquakes and floods rob us of livelihood. And God uses these trials to perfect us, even as He takes evil and works it for His purposes.

Remember the story of Joseph? He was sold into slavery by his jealous brothers but rose to a position of prominence and power in Egypt. When the brothers fell into his hands, they were sure he would punish them. Joseph's reply was, "It was really God who sent me ahead of you to save people's lives" (Genesis 45:5, TEV).

When a man or woman comes into a relationship with Christ, when he or she is found "in Him," the world does not change, people do not change. But in a mysterious way, he or she is made a part of a God-system in which God works all things together for good (Romans 8:28).

Now in this life there is no intellectual *proof* that this is so. It is a paradox. We may find the Holy Spirit giving us assurance in our hearts. Our friends may even see a difference in our lives. But there is no proof that we can lay before the world outside of Christ and say, "See, this is the way it is." It is for this reason that the Bible points to the future, the "hope" that one day we will see it all.

> At present we are men looking at puzzling reflections in a mirror. The time will come when we shall see reality whole and face to face! At present all I know is a little frac-

tion of the truth, but the time will come when I shall know it as fully as God has known me! (1 Corinthians 13:12).

Trials come in all shapes and forms. They come to our person: physical, emotional failure in our own eyes, failure to be, failure to do what we believe we should. Some of us find just the process of growing older one of great trial.

Trials come in our relationships: family and friends, the rest of the body of Christ, all humankind, for "no man *is* an island," and when one part of the human race is hurt, in some way we are all hurt. "Ask not for whom the bell tolls, it tolls for thee."

The Christian understands this. We know the world is a hurting place. But we also understand that the world is not a "closed system." There is a God Who stands outside His creation Who orders the lives of men and women. His ways are not our ways, nor His thoughts our thoughts.

If we were able to completely comprehend God, He would no longer be God. I wish some of my proof-demanding friends would see that! God will be God!

What we know about Him is what He has revealed about Himself in His creation and in His Word. And in the light of that revelation, we can experience joy even as we experience trial. We are not surprised to find things in His Word that indicate that we do indeed "see through a glass darkly." But the wonderful thing about God's Word is that as we trust ourselves to it (and thus to Him), we discover that it works. It is this faith, this building faith, that is being developed. It is faith that succeeds in facing the trials.

> This means temendous joy to you, even though at present you may be temporarily harassed by all kinds of trials. This is no accident—it happens to prove your faith, which is infinitely more valuable than gold, and gold, as you know, even though it is ultimately perishable, must be purified by fire. This proving of your faith is planned to result in praise and glory and honour in the day when Jesus Christ reveals himself (1 Peter 1:6, 7).

The writers of the Bible consistently look to trial and testing as something that is, first, to be expected, and second, has a building quality about it. In contrast, joy is something much deeper than mere happiness. In the ultimate it is that marvelous sense of well-being that comes from knowing first that there is a God Who is in control of the universe and second that He is the One Who is *for* us! Joy is experienced now because of what the future will be.

When trials come, and come they will, and real they will be, we find joy in knowing that we have been through another time when God has shown the evidence of His keeping power. Faith is strengthened. Life becomes more dependent on inner peace than outward circumstances. "The man who patiently endures the temptations and trials that come to him is the truly happy man. For once his testing is complete he will receive the crown of life which the Lord has promised to all who love him" (James 1:12).

Notes

1. Some of us who live in the affluent North need to see that the world is really divided between the "haves" of the northern hemisphere and the "have-nots" of the southern. See Willy Brandt's *North-South: A Program for Survival* and Richard Barnet's *The Lean Years: Politics in the Age of Scarcity.*

4
WISDOM VERSUS FAITH

And if, in the process, any of you does not know how to meet any particular problem he has only to ask God— who gives generously to all men without making them feel guilty—and he may be quite sure that the necessary wisdom will be given him. But he must ask in sincere faith without secret doubts. For the man who doubts is like a wave of the sea, carried forward by the wind one moment and driven back the next. That sort of man cannot hope to receive anything from the Lord, and the life of a man of divided loyalty will reveal instability at every turn (James 1:5-8).

Faith says, "Trust God. He will work it out."

Wisdom says, "This is the way to do it. Go ahead and get on with it."

Which will it be? Do I act out of my wisdom, or do I act in faith? How do I know when to exercise wisdom and when to exercise faith? Where does wisdom come from? Where does faith come from?

There's the rub. There's the tension.

The Tension of Believing When We Ask for Wisdom

James tells us that if we don't have the wisdom that we need, all we have to do is ask God.[1] But then he points out that in order to receive wisdom, we need to ask in faith. First, we need faith to believe that God gives generously to all men "without making them feel foolish or guilty." Second, we need to ask without any inward reservations as to our confidence in God.

We need to have faith about God's love toward us. How often we are afraid to ask someone how to do something for fear that he or she will consider us stupid and express their feelings either in body language or in words. They may even go a step further and reproach us for asking! How many times have we become annoyed with our own children's persistent questions to the point of exasperation: "Johnny, you've asked me that ten times, and I've given you the same answer each time. Now that's *enough*!"

Contrast our responses with these responses.

> Ho, every one that thirsteth, come ye to the waters, and he that hath no money; come ye, buy, and eat; yea, come, buy wine and milk without money and without price (Isaiah 55:1, KJV).

> Ask and it will be given to you. Search and you will find. Knock and the door will be opened for you (Matthew 7:7).

There is never "That's enough!" with God. He doesn't want to load us with guilt about our inadequacies. He accepts us just as we are at every point in our lives; He's always ready to make a new beginning, to consider this the first day of a grand adventure in knowing Him better. Today really *is* the first day of the rest of your life. God does not have a rigid, inalterable plan for each one of us, a plan that if we miss it leaves us with "God's second best."[2]

The Tension of More Wisdom and Less Faith

James tells us to ask for wisdom, and not to have doubts when we ask. At first glance we might respond, "Why would anyone ask if he didn't think he would receive it?" But the human mind is a wondrous thing. It is possible to hold to seemingly contradictory beliefs and operate as if they are both true. In the same way it is possible to believe or assert propositionally in our minds that God is able and willing to give, and yet in our heart doubt that He wants to or will do it. That's why James is so practical.[3] He knows us well! "Faith without works is dead!" To hold a set of "beliefs" and not to act upon them leaves us as "double-minded men."

The difficulty is that often as we grow in wisdom (knowledge), we find less need for faith. It is a tension, if you will, between technical capability and grace. Most of us keep working at being more capable, of being able to do more things on our own. There is something built in the American culture which holds the strong individualist[4] up as an ideal to be aimed for. We keep hoping to find security in ourselves, but it is a security in our capabilities, rather than a security in our freedom to be ourselves. This is not God's wisdom!

Jesus told us to be wise as serpents but at the same time to be innocent as doves. The wisdom that comes from God's grace is open and transparent. God's wisdom says ask in all innocence. Our asking may expose our weakness or our naiveté. But God is pleased with that kind of openness.

Wisdom is more than knowledge. It includes the best use of the knowledge we have. Wisdom is a gift of God. It has the character of being revealed. When Paul writes to the Corinthians that he has not preached Christ with eloquent wisdom or clever words, he is speaking of earthly wisdom. He quotes Isaiah 29:14: "I will destroy the wisdom of the wise, and the cleverness of the clever I will thwart." "The foolishness of God is wiser than men . . ." (1 Corinthians 1:19, 25, RSV).

The Truly Wise Have "Little" Wisdom

To be truly wise is to have God's wisdom given to us. Christianity's first martyr was a man of wisdom. We read of Stephen that when he spoke, "they could not withstand the wisdom and the Spirit with which he spoke" (Acts 6:10, RSV). Peter speaks of Paul as having been given wisdom (2 Peter 3:15). Christ's disciples were promised wisdom when they were called to give witness to their belief (Luke 21:15). "Let Christ's teaching dwell in your hearts, making you rich in true wisdom" (Colossians 3:16).

Now spiritual wisdom is not something that is to be reserved for a few. There are not to be a few wise men in each local fellowship who have the necessary insight to answer all questions. Not only are church leaders expected to have wisdom (Acts 6:3), but all members of the body should expect to have "made known to us in all wisdom and insight the mystery of his will, according to his purpose which he set forth in Christ as a plan for the fulness of time, to unite all things in him, things in heaven and things on earth" (Ephesians 1:9, 10, RSV).

Here is the tension, the paradox, if you will. It is summed up by a popular song of some years ago. The writer had his ups and downs but in the end he tells us he had done it "My way!" We, too, keep hoping to find security in ourselves, to be so wise we need no faith.

A good example of how *self*-reliant we can become is what can happen to us even as we desire to be open, transparent people. The insights of psychology tell us we need to put aside our masks and to be "real." But there is such a thing as false openness. We can have an "openness" because we feel we have made it in ourselves. We can appear to be open and unthreatened by others, because we feel we have strengths in ourselves. And so rather than removing a mask, we put on another. These are the men who "trust God, but with inward reservations." They have a divided loyalty, divided between their loyalty to God and their loyalty to themselves, to their perception of their own capabilities.

James gives us a test for wisdom: "Is there some wise and understanding man among you? Then let his life be a shining example of the humility that is born of true wisdom. But if your heart is full of bitter jealousy and rivalry, then do not boast and do not deny the truth. You may acquire a certain wisdom, but it does not come from above—it comes from this world, from your own lower nature, even from the devil" (James 3:13-15).

This is why wisdom depends on faith, and yet in this life there is always a creative tension. For the wiser we become, somehow the less faith we believe we need. But the truly wise man knows how small indeed is his wisdom. "I stand amazed at the fathomless wealth of God's wisdom and God's knowledge. How could man ever understand his reasons for action, or explain his methods of working?" (Romans 11:33).

Notes

1. Phillips chooses to let "wisdom" requested refer back to the problem of testing just stated. Since the texts of the Bible have no paragraphing, we have to use our best judgment here. James may have meant to start a new idea. I prefer Phillips's understanding of the passage.

2. I agree with Garry Friesen that God does *not* have a particular will for each of us. See his *Decision Making and the Will of God*.

3. The late Frank Gaebelein, headmaster emeritus of the Christian prep school where I first met Jesus, entitled his 1955 commentary, *The Practical Epistle of James*.

4. See my *Whatever Happened to Commitment?* for more on this. Also consult Florovsky's *Christianity and Culture* and Niebuhr's *Christ and Culture*.

5
DON'T DOUBT WHEN YOU PRAY

For the man who doubts is like a wave of the sea, carried forward by the wind one moment and driven back the next. That sort of man cannot hope to receive anything from the Lord, and the life of a man of divided loyalty will reveal instability at every turn (James 1:6-8).

For many years I found myself closing all of my prayers with the phrase, "If it be Your will. . . ." I don't know how I began that habit. Somewhere back there someone probably told me I should always pray for God's will, and this seemed like the right answer. After all, who am I to tell God what to do?

At first glance this might seem to be a very appropriate and a very pious statement. And later on when we consider God's purpose versus people's plan (chapter 15), we will make the point that we need to see all of our plans as being dependent upon God's will for us.

But I suspect that for me, this "If it be Your will . . ." was a form of Christian cop-out. I prayed for so many things to happen. Some were vast in their scope. And many of them, I had to admit, were beyond my experience and my expectation. In addition, I discovered that a number of the good things for which I prayed did not turn out. They didn't happen as I asked. I would pray for someone who was very ill that he might be healed, only to see him die. I would pray that people would come to know the Lord, only to

35

discover that they moved further away from Him. My "If it be Your will . . ." was a very pragmatic sort of thing. It got me (or God!) off the hook.

Double-Mindedness and Prayer

So how difficult it was to be confronted by these verses in James! The New International Version states it this way: "But when he asks, he must believe and not doubt, because he who doubts is like a wave of the sea, blown and tossed by the wind. That man should not think he will receive anything from the Lord; he is a double-minded man, unstable in all he does" (James 1:6-8).

Wasn't my "If it be Your will . . ." being double-minded?

What a tension *that* is!

A double-minded man! How is it possible to be a double-minded man? How is it that I can "believe" two things at the same time, two things which obviously don't fit together? My intellect says that it can't be. A thing is not A and B at the same time. How foolish to state in one breath that I am on my way home and in the next sentence to say I am leaving home.

It certainly feels like a contradiction, paradox. But it's not Christian paradox. It's human paradox: I *can* act as though I believe two contrary things at the same time. How? It is the result of a desire to make the world conform to my own experience, to trust my experience rather than to trust God.[1] God says *pray* in faithfulness. My experience says things don't always work out. My experience feels more real than my faith. But why aren't our prayers answered?

The Bible gives us many reasons. Peter tells us that it may be the result of our relationships within our family: "Husbands, in the same way be considerate as you live with your wives, and treat them with respect as the weaker partner and as heirs with you of the gracious gift of life, so that *nothing will hinder your prayers*" (1 Peter 3:7, NIV).

James gives us another reason: "You crave for something and don't get it; you are murderously jealous of what you can't possess yourselves; you struggle and fight with one another. You don't get what you want because you don't ask God for it. And when you do ask he doesn't give it to you, for you ask in quite the wrong spirit—you only want to satisfy your own desires" (James 4:2-3).

Jesus' disciples failed in their praying at times. One time they had attempted to cast out a demon with no results. Jesus had to do it for them. Later on they came to Him and asked why they could not cast it out. He responded, "Because of your little faith. For truly, I say to you, if you have faith as a grain of mustard seed, you will say to this mountain, 'Move from here to there,' and it will move; and nothing will be impossible to you" (Matthew 17:20-21, RSV).

We have looked at three reasons why prayers aren't answered: a failure in our family relationships, a failure of spirit, and a failure of faith. Contrast their failure statements with this positive one of Jesus: "Whatever you ask in my name, I will do it, that the Father may be glorified in the Son; if you ask anything in my name, I will do it" (John 14:13, 14, RSV).

When Prayers Aren't Answered . . .

What then are we to say when our prayers are not answered? What would a single-minded person do? There are two dimensions to the answer. The first is found in the context of the above verse from John's gospel. Jesus precedes His promise of answered prayer with another statement: "Truly, truly, I say to you, he who believes in me will also do the works that I do; and greater works than these will he do, because I go to the Father" (John 14:12, RSV).

Here comes the faith again: "He who believes in me . . ." He who has "sincere faith without secret doubts as to whether he really wants God's help or not."

But suppose I don't have that faith? Suppose I find doubt in myself. What should I do? Stop praying? The antidote for such a lack of faith is a continual asking. Jesus tried to point this out in the parable of the unrighteous judge.

> Then Jesus told his disciples a parable to show them that they should always pray and not give up. He said: "In a certain town there was a judge who neither feared God nor cared about men. And there was a widow in that town who kept coming to him with the plea, 'Grant me justice against my adversary.'
>
> "For some time he refused. But finally he said to himself, 'Even though I don't fear God or care about men, yet because this widow keeps bothering me, I will see that she gets justice, so that she won't eventually wear me out with her coming!' "
>
> And the Lord said, "Listen to what the unjust judge says. And will not God bring about justice for his chosen

ones, who cry out to him day and night? Will he keep putting them off? I tell you, he will see that they get justice, and quickly" (Luke 18:1-8a, NIV).

We may have immediate doubt, but our continued asking brings on the long-range trust in the God Who will answer. To be double-minded is to doubt that God will answer in our favor. To be double-minded is to be loyal to two standards. To be double-minded is to be dependent upon one's experience, even while one depends upon God.

Some may immediately ask, "Haven't you said that we can depend on our experience? What else is there to be dependent upon?"

How subtle the mind! How skillful the Tempter! God's Word is the standard. My experience may confirm or deny that Word. Where it confirms it, my faith is strengthened. Where experience appears to oppose God's Word, we move ahead believing God's Word and expecting future experience will confirm it.

"If it be Your will . . ."? What is good, what is righteous, what is just is *always* God's will, for this is the very nature of His being. God's "will" for each of us may be obscure. I personally don't believe in a model of God's plan for my life.[2] But obscurity doesn't eliminate praying.

How then should I pray? In Jesus' name. Without qualification. Believing, trusting. Single-mindedly. Persistently.

But what do I do when my prayer is not answered? Fall back on God, not to indirectly accuse Him of being responsible for the unhappy outcome, but rather to thank Him that His love is unchanging, that He will work this together for good, and that we have found Him trustworthy.

Job was faced with what was certainly a disastrous situation. His children had been killed. His wealth was gone. He was physically afflicted (Job 1:1-2:10). His wife told him, "Curse God and die." Job's response was, "Shall we accept good from God, and not trouble?"

It's not easy. But the answer to tension again is faith.

Notes

1. You may immediately ask, "Hasn't he switched arguments? Wasn't he banking on his experience just a chapter or two ago?" But apprehending biblical truth by experiencing it is different from forcing the truth of our own experience back on the Bible.

2. See Garry Friesen, *Decision Making and the Will of God.*

6
IT'S GOOD TO BE POOR

The brother who is poor may be proud because God has raised him to the true riches. The rich may be proud that God has shown him his spiritual poverty. For the rich man will wither away like summer flowers. One day the sunrise brings a scorching wind; the grass withers at once and so do all the flowers—all that lovely sight is destroyed. Just as surely will the rich man and all his ways fall into the blight of decay (James 1:9-11).

Here's a short self-test questionnaire:

	Agree				Disagree
	+2	+1	0	−1	−2
I would like my children to go to college.	☐	☐	☐	☐	☐
I need a regular vacation.	☐	☐	☐	☐	☐
It would be nice to have a large enough home so we could entertain.	☐	☐	☐	☐	☐
Everyone should have medical insurance.	☐	☐	☐	☐	☐
Christians should dress well and look good.	☐	☐	☐	☐	☐
Old people should have saved enough to be independent.	☐	☐	☐	☐	☐
I honestly don't care if I have a lot of money.	☐	☐	☐	☐	☐

As I look at my life, I really don't believe that I want to be wealthy. I don't want a lot of money. But I do want to care for my children and

my wife. And it would be nice to have a home where we could enter-
tain our friends and share our witness with others. I'd like my kids
to go to college, if they want to. And as I think to the future, I do
have some dread of getting old and being dependent on others. I
would like to be able to grow old gracefully, so I guess I'd like to have
enough money to retire on.

The pressures of my job are heavy. I need to get away from it all at
least once a year. And it's quite difficult these days to get around
with one car, so there ought to be enough money to handle two.
Medical bills can be catastrophic, and so I'd like to have enough
medical insurance to handle the problems that will come along. And
if I keep wearing the same shiny suit every day, it will soon be a dis-
grace.

But I don't really want to be *rich*. I don't really care whether I have
a lot of money. I guess what I am really saying is that I don't want to
be *poor*.

The Rich, the Poor, and . . . Me

Let's change the scene for a moment. Come with me to the Judean
hillside. Matthew, a great storyteller, is narrating an engrossing account. He has a sense of the dramatic. After establishing Jesus'
kingly ancestry, he tells us about the birth of Jesus and the visit of
the Magi, the escape to Egypt and the return to Nazareth. He follows this by introducing us to John the Baptist who "came, preaching in the Desert of Judea and saying, 'Repent, for the kingdom of
heaven is near.' " He tells us of the baptism of Jesus and His temptation. The only public words of Jesus that he has narrated for us up
until now are those same words of John the Baptist, "Repent, for the
kingdom of heaven is near" (Matthew 4:17, NIV).

Now we are gathered on the mountainside, and Matthew is about
to tell us about Jesus' first public sermon. What will be His very first
words? Out of all of the things that Matthew heard Jesus say, which
ones will the Holy Spirit inspire him to write on the sacred page?

Standing around Jesus are not only His disciples, but the scribes
and Pharisees who have been blessed with enough money so that
they can leisurely study the Word of God. The poor are here, too,
the ignorant, unlearned poor. They have followed Jesus in anticipation that in Him they might find some new hope. What will Jesus
say?

"Blessed are the poor in spirit, for theirs is the kingdom of
heaven" (Matthew 5:3, RSV). Wait a minute, Jesus, You must have

that wrong. You don't mean the *poor*, do You? You mean poor in *spirit*, don't You?

Luke makes it a little bit clearer for us: "Blessed are you poor, for yours is the kingdom of God" (Luke 6:20, RSV).

But don't the rich have it so much better? Aren't the rich the ones who can afford the best seats in the synagogue? Aren't the rich the ones who have the time to really learn? What good can it be to the poor? "You must not set your heart on what you eat or drink, nor must you live in a state of anxiety. The whole heathen world is busy about getting food and drink, and your Father knows well enough that you need such things. No, set your heart on his kingdom, and your food and drink will come as a matter of course" (Luke 12:29-31).

James sums it up nicely: "Listen, my dear brothers: Has not God chosen those who are poor in the eyes of the world to be rich in faith and to inherit the kingdom he promised those who love him?" (James 2:5, NIV).

"To inherit the kingdom . . ." The coming of Christ's kingdom has begun. It is not fully here, but it has begun.[1] If I could only believe that. If I really believed that, I wouldn't be concerned for clothes and cars and medical catastrophes. God's Spirit is at work in the world! If I could only trust myself to Him.

Living in a False Reality

Christ's kingdom is like a fourth dimension that no one can see. It permeates all the world. I live in His kingdom just as surely as I am alive. But I find it so easy to step out of this heavenly realm into the culture that surrounds me. How quickly I slip from this hidden dimension into a false "reality." And here in this imitation of reality there is a world which keeps throwing out its arms to me and laughingly calling, "Get all out of life there is to get! You deserve it!"

The tension won't go away.

I didn't ask to be born into this society. I might just as easily have been born in the midst of the starving millions of the Indian subcontinent. But I'm here, and somehow I have to work my way through all this.

Somehow I have to learn to abound in all things. Somehow I need to learn to be content whatever the circumstances may be. I need to relate to the poor of this world and the rich of this world. I need to be able to relate to *myself* when I am rich and when I am poor. I find that very hard.

Paul's "I can do all things," is so easily taken out of context: "Nor do I mean that I have been in actual need, for I have learned to be content, whatever the circumstances may be. I know now how to live when things are difficult and I know how to live when things are prosperous. In general and in particular I have learned the secret of eating well or going hungry—of facing either plenty or poverty. I am ready for anything through the strength of the One who lives within me" (Philippians 4:11-13).

And I suspect that it does little good to tell some of my friends who are getting along with very little as compared to what I have, "Be glad! God has called you to true riches!" The Apostle John has a few words on that issue. "But if any one has the world's goods and sees his brother in need, yet closes his heart against him, how does God's love abide in him? Little children, let us not love in word or speech but in deed and truth" (1 John 3:17-18, RSV).

Compared to the rest of the world, I am rich.[2] I have material wealth. James tells us this is a dangerous situation. He need only point to the world around us to make his point. Wealth has a way of easily turning us from valuing life's relationships with people to valuing things, what we own, what we have acquired. Things keep us occupied just maintaining them. Money has to be protected, invested. It all takes time, time that could be spent in building up others.

All of Scripture seems to be crying out to us how dangerous riches can be. To be wealthy is to be powerful. To be wealthy is to acquire things. To be wealthy is to have leverage, an ability to get done what we want to get done.

James describes the fate of those who have given themselves over completely to becoming rich.

> And now, you men of affluence, is the time for you to weep and wail because of the miseries in store for you! Your riches are ruined, your fine clothes are moth-eaten, your gold and silver are tarnished. Yes, their very tarnish will be evidence against you, and they will burn your flesh like fire. You have made a fine pile in these last days, haven't you? But look, here is the pay of the reaper you hired and whom you never paid, and it cries out against you! And the cries of the harvesters have reached the ears of the Lord of Hosts himself. Yes, you have had a magnificent time on this earth, and have indulged yourselves to the full. You have picked out just what you wanted like soldiers looting after battle. You have con-

demned and ruined innocent men, and they are powerless to stop you (James 5:1-6)

But what of my richer friends? They need me, too. How do I relate
to them? The only benefit that James can seem to find for the rich
man is that he should be "proud that God has shown him his
spiritual poverty." What is he trying to say? Keep it in perspective. If
we grow in grace and wisdom even as we grow in material wealth,
we will see how great is our spiritual need and how little our riches
help us meet that need. To understand one's spiritual poverty is to
seek *Christ's* riches.

> Don't pile up treasures on earth, where moth and rust
> can spoil them and thieves can break in and steal. But
> keep your treasure in Heaven where there is neither
> moth nor rust to spoil it and nobody can break in and
> steal. For wherever your treasure is, your heart will be
> there too! (Matthew 6:19-20).

And so I find two attitudes which have to be held, both of which
are dependent on my willingness to do what God's Word tells me is
best, and both of which are therefore a measure of my faith and
trust. On the one hand is the attitude that what I *have*, what I own, is
only a trust to be spent for God's glory.

On the other hand is the acceptance of whatever state of "poverty" I may be in. When I have my back against the wall financially,
when I'm without a job, when life has so encompassed me that I
must of necessity place all my trust in God's lovingkindness and
good desires for me, then I can no longer depend on my material security. Of necessity I must look elsewhere.

Living in a World of Poor

But the problem has larger dimensions.

I must not only be concerned for my brothers near at hand. Somehow to some degree I'm responsible to all people.

How do we think of ourselves in relation to our brothers and sisters in the poorer churches of the world and to the people of the
world whose income is so much less than ours? It is usually not possible for us to drop out of the society in which we live. But there are
two things that we can do: (1) We can refuse to let our money become an end in itself. We can consciously decide to place some sort
of limit on the amount of money that we will permit ourselves to use
on ourselves.[3] (2) We can seek to change our society in a direction

that will be more Christ-honoring, more concerned with others than with self.[4]

We live in a day when thankfully many people are becoming more and more concerned about their lifestyle.[5] It is possible to get into endless debates about the virtues of certain kinds of foods, what kind of clothes we should wear, or what percentage of our income should be spent in different areas of our life. We can bypass all of these concerns if we limit the amount of money we have to spend on all of them! A strategy of living which places a limit on the amount of money one can acquire solves many problems.

There are a number of ways of approaching this, some more radical than others. One strategy that almost everyone can adopt is to limit the amount of additional income that one will permit himself to acquire. This can be done by either putting aside all increases in income over what we are now receiving, or to put aside, say, fifty percent of all increases.

But trying to be different in the midst of our society is an uphill battle all the way. Many have concluded it is impossible to live as an individual and stand against the tendency of our society to shape us into its mold. They believe that the only effective way is to move into communities of accountability, places where they can hold each other accountable for their own actions.[6]

But moving out beyond this, Christians need to become involved in the society that is around them. Too often we evangelicals have so separated ourselves from the world that the world does not even know we exist. How quickly we forget Jesus' statements to His disciples.

> You are the salt of the earth. But if the salt loses its saltiness, how can it be made salty again? It is no longer good for anything, except to be thrown out and trampled by men.

> You are the light of the world. A city on a hill cannot be hidden. Neither do people light a lamp and put it under a bowl. Instead they put it on its stand, and it gives light to everyone in the house. In the same way, let your light shine before men, that they may see your good deeds and praise your Father in heaven (Matthew 5:13-16, NIV).

So the tension remains: We must live in the world, work in the world, change the world, and yet not be a part of it.

The contradiction remains: Christ's kingdom has arrived and is yet to come.

I have to live and move and work in a material world. And yet my attention needs to be on another world.

And thus the tension always will be there. It's like balancing oneself in the middle of a seesaw. A step too far on the plank pushes one side hard to the ground. There we struggle—unbalanced. In order to balance the tension, each of us has to continually work through where we are and accept ourselves there. Not permanently. We are in process. We are on a journey. God has much to do with us yet.

Perhaps a worse tension is not to judge one another. (See chapter 11.) For no matter how I prayerfully work this out, there will be other Christians who feel differently. Let's agree that the Holy Spirit is not shut up to leading all of us to the same lifestyle at the same time.

One of my favorite verses from Phillips's paraphrase is Ephesians 5:15-16: "Live life, then, with a due sense of responsibility, not as men [and women!] who do not know the meaning of life but as *those who do*. Make the best use of your time, despite all the evils of these days."

Notes

1. The idea that the kingdom has already come is reflected in Matthew 12:25-28 and has been well developed by George Ladd in his *Gospel of the Kingdom*.

2. See Ron Sider, *Rich Christians in an Age of Hunger*.

3. See Sider for some suggestions.

4. Stan Mooneyham sums it up in the title of his book, *What Do You Say to a Hungry World?*

5. See Rifkin, *The Emerging Order*. Richard Quebedeaux has some hard things to say to us and about us in *The Worldly Evangelicals*.

6. See Jim Wallis's *An Agenda for Biblical People*. For comments on community living read Michael Harper, *A New Way of Living* and the late Charles Mellis's *Committed Communities: Fresh Streams for World Mission*.

7
EVIL EXISTS, BUT GOD DID NOT CREATE IT!

A man must not say when he is tempted, "God is tempting me." For God cannot be tempted by evil, and does not himself tempt anyone. No, a man's temptation is due to the pull of his own inward desires, which greatly attract him. It is his own desire which conceives and gives birth to sin. And sin when fully grown produces death—make no mistake about that, brothers of mine! But every good endowment and every complete gift must come from above, from the Father of all lights, with whom there is never the slightest variation or shadow of inconsistency. By his own wish he made us his own sons through the Word of truth, that we might be, so to speak, the first specimens of his new creation (James 1:13-18).

Paradox One: I am both good and evil.

Paradox Two: Evil exists, but God did not create it.

Paradox Three: God can use evil for good.

For most of us, "growing in Christ" is a painful experience. It's not that we don't see progress. But when in our more reflective moments we push deeper into our motivations, we find them mixed at best, both evil and good. I remember the struggle of one of my children who wanted to ask another girl to come to church with her. Patty wanted to share the Person she knew with her friend. And yet at the same time she wanted the approval of the group at church who would commend her for bringing her non-Christian friend.

What should she do? She should do that which God approves (bringing her friend closer to the Lord) *and* resist that which she also discovers in herself (seeking the approval of her friends).

The Struggle Against Evil

Here is a real tension. We are Christians. We are not supposed to sin. We do sin. God is willing to forgive us our sin as we ask His forgiveness, but after a while the whole routine seems just that, a routine; and there is that secret (and sometimes open) question, "What difference does it make? God knows I am going to sin. And maybe He's the One Who is responsible. After all, He made me this way, didn't He?"

The Apostle Paul has a way of hitting these questions head on. All through the book of Romans he raises these really tough ones. The way he phrased this question was: "One of you will say to me: 'Then why does God still blame us? For who resists his will?' But who are you, O man, to talk back to God? 'Shall what is formed say to him who formed it, "Why did you make me like this?"' Does not the potter have the right to make out of the same lump of clay some pottery for noble purposes and some for common use?" (Romans 9:19-21, NIV).

No, the struggle must go on. The tension remains. And Paul gives us an answer to this tension, too. There is a way out through Jesus Christ, our Lord.

> My own behaviour baffles me. For I find myself doing what I really loathe but not doing what I really want to do. Yet surely if I do things that I really don't want to do, I am admitting that I really agree that the Law is good. But it cannot be said that "I" am doing them at all—it must be sin that has made its home in my nature. And, indeed, I know from experience that the carnal side of my being can scarcely be called the home of good! I often find that I have the will to do good, but not the power. That is, I don't accomplish the good I set out to do, and the evil I don't really want to do I find I am always doing. Yet if I do things that I don't really want to do then it is not, I repeat, "I" who do them, but the sin which has made its home within me. My experience of the Law is that when I want to do good, only evil is within my reach. For I am in hearty agreement with God's Law so far as my inner self is concerned. But then I find another law in my bodily members, which is in continual conflict with the Law

which my mind approves, and makes me a prisoner to the law of sin which is inherent in my mortal body. For left to myself, I serve the Law of God with my mind, but in my unspiritual nature I serve the law of sin. It is an agonising situation, and who can set me free from the prison of this mortal body? I thank God there is a way out through Jesus Christ our Lord (Romans 7:15-25).

But what about the evil that is all around us?

If we refuse to admit that we are sinners, then we live in a world of illusion and truth becomes a stranger to us. But if we freely admit that we have sinned, we find him reliable and just—he forgives our sins and makes us thoroughly clean from all that is evil (1 John 1:8-9).

This is the most difficult problem of all, and one that we can only state, rather than answer—the "problem of evil." The question is, where did evil come from? It is not James's question. He affirms the fact that evil does not come down from God. It is a human question.

People reason if God had created the entire universe, if He knew the end from the beginning, then He knew that the evil was going to enter His Kingdom in one way or another and could have chosen not to allow it. Therefore He is responsible. The logic is clear. The difficulty is that the Bible flatly states that God not only does not create evil, but that He will have nothing to do with it.

But if that is the case, how can we handle it? What do we say in the face of those who accuse God of evil?

At this point we can only fall back on our trust (faith) in God. Do we find Him reliable? Will we take Him at His word?

It is only in recent years that I have been focusing in on the *last* half of chapter 11 of the book of Hebrews. In this great Faith Chapter, the writer to the Hebrews gives us many examples of people who accomplished all kinds of things by faith: Abel, Enoch, Noah, Abraham, Isaac, Jacob, Joseph, Moses. What giants of faith they were! What great things God did through them because of their faith.

But near the end of the chapter are lists of men and women who are left nameless and for whom life did not turn out so well.

Others were tortured and refused to be released, so that they might gain a better resurrection. Some faced jeers and flogging, while still others were chained and put in prison. They were stoned; they were sawed in two; they were put to death by the sword. They went about in

> sheepskins and goatskins, destitute, persecuted and mis-
> treated—the world was not worthy of them. They wan-
> dered in deserts and mountains, and in caves and holes
> in the ground. These were all commended for their faith,
> yet none of them received what had been promised (He-
> brews 11:35b-39, NIV).

These are all the "cloud of witnesses" who have gone before us. These are the ones who demonstrate to us that God is consistent.

There is no human answer to the problem of evil that will satisfy the mind of many. The Bible starts with "in the beginning," and de-picts evil (Satan) existing in that beginning.[1] And that is as far back as we have been given to know. We can speculate where Satan came from or how it was possible that evil existed in the garden, but the problem will not go away. Our ultimate trust must remain in the God who is for us. One day all evil will be removed from the world. Meanwhile, it exists, and we exist.

Tempted by Evil, Tempted to Evil

We are tempted by evil, and we are tempted to evil. The world in which we live is an evil world. It is full of human disasters that wrack the soul. We may be in the midst of a painful physical ailment, faced with the loss of a loved one, out of a job, and thus be tempted, as was Job, to "curse God and die" (Job 2:9). On the other hand, we may be tempted to evil, to commit an act that is unloving, an act opposed to the good will of God for us.

For the individual the temptation to evil comes from many sources. Three sources that seem to be particularly clear are (1) Satan, who "prowls around like a roaring lion, seeking some one to devour" (1 Peter 5:8, RSV)[2]; (2) the circumstances of our environ-ment, our very culture with all its sinful tendencies; and (3) man's "own desires" (James 1:14). We're concerned here with the last two.

The word James uses for "temptation" has little relationship with our current use of the word as synonymous with seduction. Rather, it is the idea that men are put to a test or a trial to see how they will perform. This is why James was able to tell us earlier that when these trials and temptations come into our lives, we are to welcome them. When we have passed the test, successfully resisted the temptation, we will be stronger, more useful people. The Bible tells us God tests people. Abraham was tested when he was told by God to offer up his only son, Isaac, as a sacrifice (Genesis 22:1). The difference is that God did not mean it for evil.

When we are tempted by evil or to evil, we should remember that the temptation itself is not wrong. It is the giving in to the temptation that brings forth sin. James is speaking here particularly of the inner desire (lust), and the spiritual application is universal. And it goes even further. There may be the desire for something not evil in itself, but which will lead to sin.

Exchanging Evil for Good

So we come to the third paradox that God can use evil for good. How does God use the temptation or trial to strengthen people? Evidently by making sure that Satan does not step outside the bounds that God has set for him. The story of Job is the classic example. Satan was allowed to go no further than God permitted.[3] The writers of the New Testament give us this same assurance that God is hedging the Christian about. "No temptation has come your way that is too hard for flesh and blood to bear. But God can be trusted not to allow you to suffer any temptation beyond your powers of endurance. He will see to it that every temptation has its way out, so that it will be possible for you to bear it" (1 Corinthians 10:13).

If we sin, the responsibility is ours. If we resist, our character is strengthened.

Life is full of temptations. The results of resisting are not always easy. We shouldn't look for them. In fact, Jesus tells us that we should pray not to be led into them (Matthew 6:13). But when they come, we should use them, confident in the knowledge that God is working all these things together for good.

Every day we are faced with the evil of the world and "the sin that doth so easily beset us." We see the suffering of countless millions without sufficient food, the refugees whose only possessions are the clothes on their backs, the neighbor's child (and sometimes our own) with the incurable disease. We see and pass by so many opportunities for doing good for reasons within ourselves that we just cannot fathom. We cry out with Paul. "My own behaviour baffles me. For I find myself doing what I really loathe but not doing what I really want to do" (Romans 7:15).

At times we are tempted to scream, "Too much! Too much!" At such times the Spirit quietly speaks peace to us: "God can be trusted . . ." *God can be trusted.* James tells us that not only can God be trusted, but that we can look to Him for good things. This is the other side of the coin. "But every good endowment and every complete gift must come from above, from the Father of all lights, with whom there is never the slightest variation or shadow of inconsistency" (James 1:17).

And the ultimate of all of this is that He has made us His children: "By his own wish he made us his own sons through the Word of truth, that we might be, so to speak, the first specimens of his new creation" (James 1:18).

Notes

1. I am referring of course to the fact that the account of temptation to sin comes in Genesis 3 with no prior explanation.

2. There's a note next to this message in one of my Bibles: "He (Peter) ought to know."

3. Job 1:12 and 2:6.

8
IT'S BETTER TO BE SILENT

Knowing this, then, dear brothers, let every man be quick to listen but slow to use his tongue, and slow to lose his temper. For man's temper is never the means of achieving God's true goodness (James 1:19-20).

How quick we are to speak! How eager, how anxious! We sit and "listen" to one another thinking only of what we will say next, rather than hearing and understanding what the person is saying to us. For too many of us, the "art of conversation" is the ability to work things around to say what *we* want to say. This penchant we have for manipulating others with words became so well known that one author, Eric Berne, wrote a bestseller about *The Games People Play*.

Why We Don't Listen

Let's move ahead to the third chapter of James to get his summary of what we do.

Don't aim at adding to the number of teachers, my brothers, I beg you! Remember that we who are teachers will be judged by a much higher standard.

We all make mistakes in all kinds of ways, but the man who can claim that he never says the wrong thing can consider himself perfect, for if he can control his tongue he can control every other part of his personality! Men control the movements of a large animal like the horse with a tiny bit placed in its mouth. Ships too, for all their size and the momentum they have with a strong wind behind them, are controlled by a very small rudder according to the course chosen by the helmsman. The human tongue is physically small, but what tremendous effects it can boast of! A whole forest can be set ablaze by a tiny spark of fire, and the tongue is a fire, a whole world of evil. It is set within our bodily members but it can poison the whole body, it can set the whole of life ablaze, fed with the fires of hell.

Beasts, birds, reptiles and all kinds of sea-creatures can be, and in fact are, tamed by man, but no one can tame the human tongue. It is an evil always liable to break out, and the poison it spreads is deadly. We use the tongue to bless our Lord and Father and we use the same tongue to curse our fellow-men, who are all created in God's likeness. Blessing and curses come out of the same mouth— surely, my brothers, this is the sort of thing that never ought to happen! Have you ever known a spring to give sweet and bitter water from the same source? Have you ever seen a fig-tree with a crop of olives, or seen figs growing on a vine? It is just as impossible for salt water to produce fresh (James 3:1-12).

There it is. There's the tension. "It is just as impossible for salt water to produce fresh."

Impossible. Yet we do it every day. It is so commonplace that we don't even think about it. Oh, we can excuse ourselves with Paul's words: "So I find it to be a law that when I want to do right, evil lies close at hand" (Romans 7:21, RSV).

But we as Christians should have a higher motivation. Notice James's first words in this sentence. "In view of what he has made us then, dear brothers . . ." In view of what He has made us! "By his own wish he made us his own sons through the Word of truth, that we might be, so to speak, the first specimens of his new creation" (James 1:18).

Quick to listen! Not just to hear words. Not just to understand. To listen, to know. To really listen to another is to experience a person. The world says, "Hey, look at me!" God's Word asks us to turn the world upside down, and to say, "I want to *hear* you. I want to *know* you." To be quick to listen is to be quick to want to see another, even as God sees.

Quick to listen! What an antidote for those of us who can't hold our tongue. Someone is speaking, let me be quick to listen. For if I'm concentrating on listening, then I won't be concentrating on using my tongue. The many books on transactional analysis have a lot to teach us here. If I am sure I have understood you and the context within which you are speaking, perhaps my reply will be quite different. Perhaps I will know more about you, and because I have known you, I will grow in grace myself.

A Time to Speak

Slow to use his tongue. I remember an English professor in my prep school days who tried to show us the value of holding one's tongue. "Suppose," he said, "you are at a party where the glories of the state of Alaska are being discussed by two or three people. Suppose you were a native of Alaska, but rather than enter into the conversation, you listen quietly to what others have said. Finally someone might say to you, 'Do you know anything about Alaska?' Your simple reply might be, 'Yes, I have lived there for many years.' The next time you're in a conversation with these same people, your silence will be taken for great wisdom."

Phillips says it well when he paraphrases "slow to anger" as "slow to lose his temper." There is such a thing as righteous anger. Jesus was righteously angry when He cleansed the temple (Mark 11:15-17). There are a lot of things in this world to be angry about. When I see millions of hungry and malnourished people in the world, I get angry. When I see the political systems of the world twist and deform people's lives, I get angry. I feel. I hurt. Rightfully so. The difficulty is that my righteous anger is often quickly overshadowed by very unrighteous anger. Slow to anger, my brother, slow to anger, my sister.

But the perverseness of man is such that we even *allow* ourselves to lose our temper. Too often we use our position, particularly as parents, to find occasions to lose our temper. I graphically remember as a young father admitting myself to the luxury of losing my temper with my children. I'm sure that many times it was nothing they had done. Rather it was all of the things that had been bottled up in me at the office where it was not politic for me to lose my temper.

To lose one's temper is in one sense to lose one's "self." I am no longer me. I have allowed some demon to take charge. It is almost as though the person in whom the Spirit of God dwells has knowingly given himself or herself away. Quite rightfully James tells us that man's temper is never the means of achieving God's true goodness.

So there we have it. The contradiction is so commonplace that we don't even recognize it as a contradiction anymore.

So what's the point? Being "slow to speak" does not mean not to speak at all. There are times to speak. There are times to share the good news of salvation and Christ. There are times to speak a word of encouragement. There are times to speak of our love for one another.

But before we do, let's make certain that we have listened.[1]

Notes

1. And if you need some practice, try *The Awesome Power of the Listening Ear* by John Drakeford.

9
LIBERTY AS A LAW

Have done, then, with impurity and every other evil which overflows into the lives of others, and humbly accept the message that God has planted in your hearts, and which can save your souls. Don't only hear the message, but put it into practice; otherwise you are merely deluding yourselves. The man who simply hears and does nothing about it is like a man catching the reflection of his natural face in a mirror. He sees himself, it is true, but he goes off without the slightest recollection of what sort of person he saw in the mirror. But the man who looks into the perfect law, the law of liberty, and makes a habit of so doing, is not the man who hears and forgets. He puts that law into practice and wins true happiness.

If anyone appears to be "religious" but cannot control his tongue, he deceives himself and we may be sure that his religion is useless. Religion that is pure and genuine in the sight of God the Father will show itself by such things as visiting orphans and widows in their distress and keeping oneself uncontaminated by the world (James 1:21-27).

People think of Christianity in many ways. To some people it is the religion of their parents. ("I've always been a Christian.") To others it is the religion of the United States. ("What do you think I am, a *Buddhist*?") Some have gone further and can look back on the time when they made a commitment of their will to God, recognizing their need for His forgiveness and accepting the saving forgiveness available in Jesus Christ. ("I accepted Christ when I was nine years old.")

And then there are those who in some ways are still accepting Him. Not that they didn't make a one time, once-and-for-all decision for Christ. No, it's rather that they see that there is always more to learn about Him. These are they who continually "look into the perfect law of liberty."

A Propositional Faith

When I was thirteen I attended a Christian prep school and in a very natural manner invited Christ to enter my life. I think I imagined at that time that as I "grew in grace" I would draw closer and closer to the Father. What actually happened was quite a different thing. The more I allowed the Holy Spirit to operate within my life, the deeper became my understanding of His majesty, glory, and power. As my knowledge increased, so did my understanding of the tremendous gap that yawned between where I am and where He is. I began with a small intellectual understanding and moved on by experiencing Him.

Jesus faces us with the difference between a "propositional faith," one that merely accepts a set of statements as being true, and a trusting faith, one which says, "If that is so, then this is what I must do." James wants us to face up to the fact that *if* we have "humbly accepted this message that God has sown in your hearts, and which can save your souls," it will become operational. We will put it into practice.

By the way, we could immediately conclude from this that if we start to do this or that or such-and-such a thing, this will save our soul. No, it is Christ's grace that has the saving ability. The actions demonstrate what has happened. But back to James's true faith.

It is all too easy to have a propositional faith, a faith which focuses all its attention on what transpired in the past. Our American penchant for "facts" and "truth" often causes us to focus on ideas rather than actions. Our faith is a series of things which we affirm rather than a statement of how we *live out* our lives.[1] James compares that kind of faith to a man who has glanced once into a passing mirror. He saw his reflection. For a moment he saw himself as one of God's chosen people, destined for a life of love. But then he passes on and forgets. He forgets that although he is free from the law of sin and

58

death, he has now become a bondservant to a new law, the law of love, the perfect law of liberty.

Two observations are important here: (1) No one knows when (the moment) someone is saved, when he or she becomes indwelt by God's Spirit and thus becomes a child of God. Because this is true, we need to be very careful about establishing a cause/effect relationship between when and how a person hears the message and when it takes root.[2] (2) It follows that what happens *after* a verbal acceptance may be used by the Holy Spirit to complete the transaction. That is why some "step of faith" is so helpful to the new believer. If no action follows verbal commitment, if there is no break with "impurity and every other evil that touches the lives of others," then James says it is as though we just caught a passing glimpse in a mirror of what we might have been.

The Trap of "Having Arrived"

The question here is not how we are saved, but the tension of sanctification, the tension of growing in grace—of "becoming." For it is a tension. There is always the inertia of wanting to continue as we are or to believe that we have spiritually arrived. We never have.

How do we keep out of this trap? "The man who looks into the perfect law, the law of liberty, *and makes a habit of so doing* is not the man who hears and forgets. He puts that Law into practice and wins true happiness."

Orlando Costas talks about the need for a series of conversions. To be converted is to turn about and move in another direction. Costas talks of the need for an initial conversion to Christ, to stop walking away from Him and to put our trust in Him. Then he sees a need for us to be converted to the church, to take responsibility for ourselves as members of the body of Christ. Another conversion is a conversion to the world, to take responsibility for the world in which we live and to become the salt and light that we are called to become. This is being converted to the law of liberty.[3]

What is this law of liberty? Are we back in bondage to another law? How can there be both law and liberty? "You are no longer living under the Law, but under grace" (Romans 6:14).

But as we noted in James 1:1, as James saw his relationship to his earthly brother, Jesus, we too have accepted the role of bondservant to God. And the freedom that we are given is the freedom to love and to serve God and men. "When you were slaves to sin, you were free from the control of righteousness. What benefit did you reap at that time from the things you are now ashamed of? Those things result in death! But now that you have been set free from sin and have become slaves to God, the benefit you reap leads to holiness, and the result is eternal life" (Romans 6:20-22, NIV).

At first glance, this may not seem like much of a freedom. But the ability to love, and to receive love in return, to live in relationship with God and man in such a way that builds into our own lives—this is the greatest of gifts.

Paul writes in Galatians 6:2, "Carry each other's burdens and so live out the law of Christ." This is the "law of liberty" of which James also writes. Both are the freedom to love. "It is to freedom that you have been called, my brothers. Only be careful that freedom does not become mere opportunity for your lower nature. You should be free to *serve each other in love*. For after all, the whole Law toward others is summed up by this one command, 'Thou shalt love thy neighbour as thyself' " (Galatians 5:13, 14).

The Freedom of Being Bound

And so the tension remains. The world tells us that freedom is meant to make us independent. God says He gives us freedom to be servants of one another. And the more we love and serve one another, strangely, the more we are free.

The paradox grows deeper. Christ gives a new freedom, sets us free from death, but also sets us free to love. The more we submit to the law of liberty, the law of love—rather than just snatching a passing glimpse in the mirror—the more able we are to love and be loved. And the freer we are.

> If you obey the royal Law, expressed by the scripture, "Thou shalt love thy neighbor as thyself", all is well. But once you allow any invidious distinctions to creep in, you are sinning, you stand condemned by that Law. Remember that a man who keeps the whole Law but for a single exception is none the less a law-breaker. The one who said, "Thou shalt not commit adultery" also said, "Thou shalt do no murder". If you were to keep clear of adultery but were to murder a man you would have become a breaker of the whole Law.

> Anyway, you should speak and act as men who will be judged by the law of freedom. The man who makes no allowances for others will find none made for him. Mercy may laugh in the face of judgment (James 2:8-13).

Notes

1. See Edward Stewart, *American Cultural Patterns: A Cross-Cultural Perspective*.

2. Few Americans recognize that the idea that every "effect" must have a "cause" is a strange way of looking at things for most people in the world. See *American Cultural Patterns: A Cross-Cultural Perspective*.

3. For more vintage Costas, read the *The Church and Its Mission: A Shattering Critique from the Third World*.

10
CULTURE VERSUS CHRISTIANITY

Don't ever attempt, my brothers, to combine snobbery with faith in our glorious Lord Jesus Christ! Suppose one man comes into your meeting well-dressed and with a gold ring on his finger, and another man, obviously poor, arrives in shabby clothes. If you pay special attention to the well-dressed man by saying "Please sit here—it's an excellent seat", and say to the poor man, "You stand over there, or if you must sit, sit on the floor by my feet", doesn't that prove that you are making class-distinctions in your mind, and setting yourselves up to assess a man's quality from wrong motives? For do notice, my dear brothers, that God chose poor men, whose only wealth was their faith, and made them heirs to the kingdom promised to those who love him. And if you behave as I have suggested, it is the poor man that you are insulting. Look around you. Isn't it the rich who are always trying to rule your lives, isn't it the rich who drag you into litigation? Isn't it usually the rich who blaspheme the glorious name by which you are known? (James 2:1-7).

Will it be Christianity or our culture? Can they coexist?[1]

The difference between the world's standards and God's standards seems to be most clearly defined right here. The world, at least our Western world, says it is what you *have* that counts. God says it is what you *are*, the quality of inner life, that is important. How often have we heard that men look on the outward appearance, but God looks on the heart. It is true, my brothers. It is true, my sisters! Western culture demands a hierarchy of goods; Christianity claims a fellowship among people.

It is not necessarily true that the rich man is poor in faith, nor that the man strong in faith may not be rich. But experience shows that it takes a lot of time and hard work to acquire wealth (barring a rich uncle!), and as we have already noted, where your mind is, where your time is spent, your heart is likely to follow.

The Culture of Winners and Beauties

As we face into this question of Christianity versus culture, we need to be specific. Which culture? As North Americans we need to understand how different our culture is from most of those in the rest of the world. It's not that their cultures are alike and ours is different. Rather, it is the fact that on any scale of cultural values, North Americans seem to be at one end.

In recent years there have been a rash of books, both Christian and secular, that talk about the impact of our culture in shaping our values and in shaping how we act out our Christianity.[2] Most of these talk about the impact of American ethical or moral values on our Christian values. But we need to get underneath what is often merely the evidence of another value.

First, a look at some values. As we have noted earlier, Americans are very cause and effect oriented. We believe that there must be reason for everything happening. On another tack, Americans love to compare things. While a Chinese will say the American way is good and the Chinese way is good, the American typically will say the American way is better (or perhaps the Chinese way is better). And then the premier value in American culture is individualism, the idea that the individual is independent of the rest of society and should be "whole" within himself or herself.

All of these values—cause and effect orientation, the love of comparison, individualism—work themselves out in some interesting ways. Take, for example, comparison, and its ugly counterpart hiding underneath—snobbery. Snobbery is one man saying to another, "I'm better than you." It comes in all forms (including spiritual). How natural it is. For how can I know that I'm good, we reason, if I'm not *better*? And how can I be better if I'm not better than someone else? Everything seems to be relative, comparative.

"My, he's handsome." (Translation: He's better looking than most men I know.)

"Doesn't she have a beautiful voice?" (Translation: Her voice is much better than most of the voices I've heard.)

Inwardly we know that there's something wrong with this system, but even as we attempt to substitute a pass-fail system for comparative grades in school, even as we try to reduce some of the competition of children's sports, there's a cultural self to us. We all love a "winner."

We've already talked about wealth in terms of the rich and the poor (chapter 6). But what about wealth in relative terms? When is someone better?[3]

It doesn't have to be a lot of wealth to make a difference. Most of us don't have the opportunity to associate with very many truly wealthy people. (There aren't that many to go around.) But if you have a job which permits you a certain amount of freedom, freedom to have vacations, a second car, weekends away, and your brother is having a hard time meeting the mortgage payments on his small home, there is a difference in wealth that is considerable. How easy it is to fall into the trap of wanting to be with people who do the same things, people who naturally have "a lot to talk about." This is what James is talking about.

It's really our *Christianity against our culture.* And so often the two don't mix any better than oil and water.

But here is the other tension; the paradox, if you will. Christianity is always found *in* a culture.

Christianity, Culture, and Tension

When the gospel comes to a new culture, it stands in judgment on that culture. Some aspects of that culture must go if they stand over and against the biblical norms. Others can be transformed. A good example of the latter would be the utilization of the Christmas tree as a Christian symbol. Finally, there are those cultural norms which are not only biblically valid, but need to be held up as good.

On the other hand, there is no such thing as Christianity apart from culture. How our faith works itself out in practical living will be dependent upon the culture within which it must operate. This is no easy matter. Because most of us have been brought up to live within the society in which we are now living, most of us have only experienced Christianity in the context of this society. We easily assume that the way we do things is normative, that this is the way it *should* be done by all Christians in all settings. It takes hard work to think and pray our way to a cultural understanding.

Let's take a look at some of the forces that are creating the tension between Christianity changing culture and Christianity living in culture.

First, we live in a society which is dominated by what Jacques Ellul calls *technique*,[4] but which we usually think of as technology. Ellul's word is perhaps better because it helps us to see that technology is not just spacesuits and TV sets. It is lipstick, disposable diapers, freeways, aluminum foil, Formica kitchen cabinets, polyester clothing, styrofoam Christmas ornaments, home computers, nylon lingerie, Hot Wheels toy cars, Bisquick—you name it. It is impossible for us to "get back to nature." We left it long ago. As long as we live in North America as it is presently arranged, these "things" are going to have an impact on how we live, and even on how we think about the way we live.[5]

Second, Christianity is not against technology or technique as such. It is against a value system that places a higher value on things than people, or a higher value on people who possess a lot of things. We have much to learn about values, as we shall see.

Third, there are no sinful things. There are only sinful people who use things for sinful means or ends. But to be surrounded by things is to be tempted to a view of self which easily omits the need for others, *or* God.

Fourth, our Western society is not anywhere near as homogeneous as most of us believe. It is made up of hundreds of subcultures—regional, ethnic, occupational, religious, social, economic, plus a wide range of lesser factors, both alone and in different combinations. It continues to subdivide into smaller groups.[6] In our attempts to overcome the resulting feeling of estrangement with the world around us, we keep seeking "people like us" with whom we can feel comfortable. We have only to observe the homogeneity of the average local church to see the result.[7]

Fifth, our Western "rugged individualism" is a drastic departure from the way God intended society to be. Part of what happens to us as we become Christians is that we have potentially new relationships with other people. We are no longer seen as individuals, but as part of a human-like body. Just as each of us has one body with many members, and these members do not all have the same function, so in Christ, we who are many form one body and each member belongs to all the others (Romans 12:4, 5, RSV).

Sixth, Christianity claims—and has demonstrated for hundreds of years—that it is not only cross-cultural, but that it can overcome the barriers of cultural difference between people living in the same geographic location. But most of us have never had the experience of seeing Christianity impregnate a new culture, let alone see it break down the cultural barriers. People who are "not like us" frighten us.⁸

Honoring the Less Honorable

Having said all this, where are we? How can we avoid the trap of social snobbery? How can we find a balance between the need to live in the culture in which we find ourselves and still be obedient to God's Word?

We obviously start with values. God has said that your poor brother (or your rich brother) is of value. In fact, the Bible assumes a greater value for the faith of the poor man and a lesser value for the faith of a rich man. ("It is easier for a camel to go through the eye of a needle than for a rich man to enter the kingdom of God" [Matthew 19:24, RSV].) When all the earthly props are gone, we finally come to understand where our ultimate support lies. So we keep working on that understanding. And if we could learn to like this one tension, everything else would probably fall into place.

What are your values? Where does your "treasure" lie? More and more we are coming to understand that our values are not determined by what we believe, but by what we do.

Try this. Make a list of all of the things that you really like to do. Now write them on some kind of an A, B, C scale. Put an A in front of all the ones you like to do very much, a B in front of all of those you like to do, and a C in front of all those you like to do the least.

What do your "A" values tell you about yourself?

Or try this: Make a list of all the commitments that you have. List everything you can think of: commitments to your family, commitments to the bank, commitments to whose to whom you owe money, commitments to those to whom you've made promises to do things. What does this tell you about your real values?

What have you done to discover why God loves this or that brother or sister as much as he does? If God loves her, she is loved by the greatest Person in the universe.

What are you teaching your children in this area? What do they hear you talk about at the dinner table? What kind of friends do they see you having? What actions do they see you taking as a family to reach across these artificial social barriers to others? What kind of people do they see you consistently working to help? What does your attitude about what you are doing say to them? Are you leading from strength or from weakness?[8]

On the positive side is the need to do good to all men, especially those who are of the household of faith (Galatians 6:10). Which means that we had better be quietly thinking about ways to build each other up both socially and materially. And perhaps an even greater joy is learning to be the *recipients* of others' concern.

Near the end of the passage in 1 Corinthians 12 on our relationship to one another, Paul gives us these words: "The eye cannot say to the hand 'I don't need you!' And the head cannot say to the feet, 'I don't need you.' On the contrary, those parts of the body that seem to be weaker are indispensable, and the parts that we think are less honorable we treat with special honor . . ." (1 Corinthians 12:21-23a, NIV).

". . . and the parts we think are less honorable we treat with special honor." Think of all the people that you consider your friends or people you know in your local church. Which of these would you consider the least deserving of honor? What would happen if we started treating these who are least deserving of honor with as much honor as we possibly could? First, we would have to get to know them so that we could honor them honestly. But then, as you and others within your local fellowship began to honor these people, what would happen? Why, they would become more honored! How different this is from our normal way of thinking. We usually want to give honor to those who are at the top of the heap.

But imagine what might happen as those deserving less honor were more and more honored. Your local fellowship would become very much like a spring that was bubbling up from hidden resources. What a new dimension that would give to living!

Christianity exists within culture. It exists to transform men, women, and institutions, to make them over in the image of their culture. The world wants to shape us into its mold.

Don't let it.

Notes

1. For a good overview of the question, see Richard Niebuhr, *Christ and Culture*.

2. See Rifkin, Quebedeaux, Lasch, and Dayton.

3. John Gardner asks the same question in the subtitle of his landmark book, *Excellence*. Can we be equal and excellent too?

4. Ellul, Jacques, *Technological Society*.

5. See Peter Berger, et al, in *The Homeless Mind* for the impact our technological thinking has on the average Westerner. Also Daniel Bell's *The Cultural Contradictions of Capitalism*.

6. See Michael Novak, *The Rise of the Unmeltable Ethnics*. For an understanding of "people groups," see my *That Everyone May Hear*.

7. It has been argued that such homogeneity is needed to make a local church grow. I am aware of the pragmatic fact but am not so certain of the biblical principle. For some help here, read Elizabeth O'Connor's *The Eighth Day of Creation*. On the other hand, any group of people who stay together for any length of time *will* become homogeneous!

8. Ted Engstrom and I have tried to be of help in this area with our book *Strategy for Living*.

11
TO JUDGE OR NOT TO JUDGE

Anyway, you should speak and act as men who will be judged by the law of freedom. The man who makes no allowances for others will find none made for him. Mercy may laugh in the face of judgment (James 2:12b-13).

I suspect that if there is one area of my life with which I have the most difficulty, it is in this area of judging. To judge is to evaluate, to decide if something is right or wrong, better or worse. How quickly I judge!

"It would have been much better if they had done it this way."

"I can't imagine a Christian doing anything like that!"

"Why, that's *wrong!*"

Now it is easy to argue that this is just part of my background and training. After all, I was trained as an engineer and scientist, and then in mid-life I went through the process of a strongly academic seminary education. I should evaluate things . . . shouldn't I?

If it were just a matter of judging things, perhaps it would be all right. The difficulty is that what I am doing is judging people, and too often those people are my brothers and sisters in Christ.

"But we *have* to judge," you may reply. "We have to choose. We have to decide. After all, don't we keep hearing sermons about choosing the good over the better and the best over the good?"

Ah, there's the tension again. We have to, and yet we mustn't. How do we handle this one?

The Judgments of the Strong and the Weak

One of the most interesting responses to all of this comes from the Apostle Paul as he writes to the Corinthians and the Romans about eating meat that is offered to idols. The problem was a common one. In the pagan cities in which the early Christians found themselves, the priests of many temples disposed of their excess offerings through the local meat market. On the one hand, it was meat just like any other meat; in fact, it might have even been of higher quality. On the other hand, it was meat that had been offered as part of an idol's sacrifice. Should one eat this meat or not? And what about fellow Christians who did? What should we say to them?

> "Everything is permissible"—but not everything is beneficial. "Everything is permissible"—but not everything is constructive. Nobody should seek his own good, but the good of others.
>
> Eat anything sold in the meat market without raising questions of conscience, for, "The earth is the Lord's, and everything in it."
>
> If some unbeliever invites you to a meal and you want to go, eat whatever is put before you without raising questions of conscience. But if anyone says to you, "This has been offered in sacrifice," then do not eat it, both for the sake of the man who told you and for conscience' sake—the other man's conscience, I mean, not yours. For why should my freedom be judged by another's conscience? (1 Corinthians 10:23-29, NIV).

Paul has gone over the same ground in the eighth chapter of 1 Corinthians and summed it up by saying, "Therefore, if food is a cause of my brother's falling, I will never eat meat, lest I cause my brother to fall."

Now, that all seems straightforward. If I am the "stronger brother," then I should act like one.

But turn with me to Romans 14 where Paul is dealing with a similar subject.

> Accept him whose faith is weak, without passing judgment on disputable matters. One man's faith allows him to eat everything, but another man, whose faith is weak, eats only vegetables. The man who eats everything must not look down on him who does not, and the man who does not eat everything must not condemn the man who does, for God has accepted him. Who are you to judge someone else's servant? To his own master he stands or

falls. And he will stand, for the Lord is able to make him stand (Romans 14:1-4, NIV).

There we have it. My response to my weaker brother is not in response to his judgment, but in response to his need. The response of my weaker brother when he sees me eating meat is not to judge me, but to see me as a fellow traveler in Christ who one day will stand side-by-side with him before the Judge of the universe.

> Therefore let us stop passing judgment on one another. Instead, make up your mind not to put any stumbling block or obstacle in your brother's way. As one who is in the Lord Jesus, I am fully convinced that no food is unclean in itself. But if anyone regards something as unclean, then for him it is unclean. If your brother is distressed because of what you eat, you are no longer acting in love. Do not by your eating destroy your brother for whom Christ died. Do not allow what you consider good to be spoken of as evil. For the kingdom of God is not a matter of eating and drinking, but of righteousness, peace and joy in the Holy Spirit, because anyone who serves Christ in this way is pleasing to God and approved by men (Romans 14:13-18, NIV).

How easy it is to write those words. How difficult to carry them out. After all, don't I have rights? If I am part of Christ's body, don't I have some privileges within that body? Must I continually keep deferring to others? Evidently the answer is yes, for James tells us to "Never pull each other to pieces, my brothers. If you criticise your brother and judge your brother you have become in fact a critic and judge of the Law. Yet if you start to criticise the Law instead of obeying it you are setting yourself up as judge. There is only one judge, the One who gave the Law, to whom belongs absolute power of life and death. How can you then be your neighbour's judge?" (James 4:11-12).

Is that all there is to it? Are there no ways that we can help one another to be built together into the body of Christ, ways that will give us unity of mind and spirit without judging one another?

In the examples we have given above, Paul was judging actions of others about which there could be honest differences of opinion. He was assuming that we serve the same God and (indirectly) that we have the same Word of God as our authority.

He was not saying, however, that all of life is relative. To commit adultery is wrong. It is a sin. To steal from another is wrong. It is a sin. To lie to one another is wrong. It is a sin. But even as we judge these things to be wrong, and therefore indirectly judge the one who committed them as sinning, we need to realize that God's forgiveness is always available, and as God forgives this person, he or she is *completely* forgiven, a new creature with a past blotted out from God's mind.

What About Honest Differences of Opinion?

But what about honest differences of opinion? What about the need for evaluating, as might be the case in trying to select a new pastor for our church or evaluating someone's performance on the job? How do we handle situations like this?

One of the interesting phenomena of our day is how much more time the world spends in thinking about the needs of individuals than do most Christians. The world is continually searching for ways to get along with one another, to understand a psychology of man.[1] We should not be surprised that much of what is being done is extremely biblical. For the system the world is seeking to learn about is the same system described in God's Word.

A great deal of study has gone into the whole question of managing conflict, of managing differences between people. It has been recognized that in the settlement of most differences, somebody wins and somebody loses. The one who wins may feel great, but what about the one who loses? Do we always have to have win/lose situations, or could we not have win/win situations?

The approach that has been adopted by Rensis Likert[2] and others is to be so accepting of others as persons that the difference between them is viewed as something outside the two persons, something which two people or two groups can work together on for a solution that is acceptable to both. True, the apostles of this form of humanism see it as resulting in a utopian society in which we have complete freedom as we have complete mastery. As Christians, we know too much about fallen human nature to believe in such an ultimate triumph. But the goal is a good goal. The desire is a good desire.

So we can learn here. As Christians we need to evaluate situations, not people. As members of Christ's body, we need to believe that God intends us to have the kind of unity described in His Word.

Finally, we need to realize that we will continually be placed in situations where we have to choose between two courses of action, and many times between two people. How do we handle this? James tells us: "You should speak and act as men who will be judged by the law of freedom." What is this law of freedom? As we pointed out in chapter 9, the law of freedom, the law of liberty, is the law which makes us consider the other person's interest first and become bondservants of one another.

Within our Christian fellowship and in our relationship with all men, we need to keep pressing on to what is right, even as we acknowledge the fact that righteousness will not fill the earth until the Son of Man returns. "Don't make complaints against each other in the meantime, my brothers—you may be the one at fault yourself. The judge himself is already at the door" (James 5:9).

Notes

1. We are even to the point of being called *The Psychological Society!* by Martin Gross. In *Stress Without Distress*, Hans Selye says the way to reduce your own stress is to be kind to everyone so they will continually be kind to you. Does sound biblical, doesn't it?

2. Rensis and Jane Likert, *New Ways of Managing Conflict*.

12
FAITH NEEDS WORKS,
WORKS NEED FAITH

Now what use is it, my brothers, for a man to say he "has faith" if his actions do not correspond with it? Could that sort of faith save anyone's soul? If a fellow man or woman has no clothes to wear and nothing to eat, and one of you say, "Good luck to you. I hope you'll keep warm and find enough to eat", and yet give them nothing to meet their physical needs, what on earth is the good of that? Yet that is exactly what a bare faith without a corresponding life is like—quite dead. A man could challenge us by saying, "You have faith and I have merely good actions. Well, all you can do is to show me a faith without corresponding actions, but I can show you by my actions that I have faith as well."

So you believe that there is one God? That's fine. So do all the devils in hell, and shudder in terror! For, my dear short-sighted man, can't you see far enough to realise that faith without the right actions is dead and useless? Think of Abraham, our ancestor. Wasn't it his action which really justified him in God's sight when his faith led him to offer his son Isaac on the altar? Can't you see that his faith and his actions were, so to speak, partners— that his faith was implemented by his deed? That is what the scripture means when it says:

And Abraham believed God,
And it was reckoned unto him for righteousness;
And he was called the friend of God.

A man is justified before God by what he does as well as by what he believes. Rahab, who was a prostitute, has been quoted as an example of faith, yet surely it was her action that pleased God, when she welcomed Joshua's reconnoitering party and sent them safely back by a different route.

Yes, faith without action is as dead as a body without a soul (James 2:14-26).

At the time of the Reformation, Luther brought a very necessary corrective to the life of the Church. His ringing cry from Galatians that "a man is not justified by works of the law but through faith in Jesus Christ . . ." (2:16, RSV) rose like a dam to stop the swelling tide of a Christianity that was engrossed in getting to heaven by its own acts of righteousness. But the corrective of the Reformation tended to cover a truth that is just as real—there is no such thing as a true faith that does not produce some action that others can see.

When Actions Must Jibe with Words

I sometimes like to shock a good evangelical congregation by announcing rather strongly, "I don't really care what you believe. I'm more interested in what you *do!*" But it's true, isn't it? You and I really are much more interested in what people do than in what they believe. And if what they do does not jibe with what they say they believe, we are quick to redefine for them what they really believe.

Well, what is it, faith or works? Believe or do? Or is it both? (But how can that be?) Part of our difficulty is our "Greek mind," the mind which sees a compartmentalized world, a world divided between the physical and the spiritual. Today it might better be called a Western technological mind.

Again, we are trapped in our culture. We don't know that we are using Western technological thought when we approach the Bible, because that's the way most people in our culture think. And because the people around us think that way, we go on to assume that all men think that way, *including* God.

We must be rational. Two plus two must still equal four, mustn't it?

So we go our way, dividing up the world into the intellectual, the emotional, the spiritual, the physical, and a hundred other dimensions as though it were possible for the world to be divided up that way. We fail to see that although these are useful categories for thinking about the world, life refuses to conform to our categories and our rational thought. And God's ways often rise above our categories.

We are justified by faith, and faith alone.

Yet a faith without works is dead. It was never alive. It is no-faith.

There are many simple analogies. If you plug in an electric drill to a wall socket and the drill fails to work, you are quick to surmise that there is no electricity. The evidence of the existence of electricity is power emanating through the drill. The evidence of the existence of faith is the works seen in life.

So much for the apparent paradox. Two tensions remain.

(1) How can I be certain that what I'm doing is not "just to prove" that I believe (have faith)?

(2) How can I demonstrate to myself that I really believe when I'm displeased at my actions? ("If I really trusted Christ, wouldn't I be doing thus-and-so?")

Finding Help by Finding Failure

These are real tensions. It would be an unusual person who has never experienced them. To make matters worse, almost all of us find that our actions all fall short of our professed faith. There are many more good things we ought to do than we are able to do. Daily we are faced with too many oughts.

Paul certainly faced this same dilemma in himself:

> So I find this law at work: When I want to do good, evil is right there with me. For in my inner being I delight in God's law; but I see another law at work in the members of my body, waging war against the law of my mind and making me a prisoner of the law of sin at work within my members. What a wretched man I am! Who will rescue me from this body of death? (Romans 7:21-24, NIV).

We need to begin with Paul's answer: "Thanks be to God—through Jesus Christ our Lord!" (v. 25). Thanks be to God He understands all of these things. He knows me.

> You know when I sit and when I rise;
>   you perceive my thoughts from afar.
> You discern my going out and my lying down;
>   you are familiar with all my ways.
> Before a word is on my tongue
>   you know it completely, O LORD (Psalm 139:2-4, NIV).

In the midst of all of our failure God is the One who is for us!

A number of things have been of help to me here. The first has been to realize that much of life is "failure." It took me a long time to come to that discovery, but then one day I realized that the best baseball player I knew "failed" six times out of ten. For every ten times that he went to bat, he only hit the ball four. Sin is "missing the mark." A 3.95 average in college is "sin." We have missed the mark. This helped me to realize that although God has given me a standard ("Be ye perfect [complete], therefore, as your Heavenly Father is perfect" [Matthew 5:48].) against which to measure myself, God is much more interested in my successes than in my failures.

Second is the marvelous thought that "as far as the east is from the west, so far does he remove our transgressions from us" (Psalm 103:12, RSV).

The Lord does not see my past. He has put my failure to measure up completely behind me.

This brings me to the third help, the blessed hope that lies before me, a hope that one day all will be right. And it is because of this blessed hope and because each day I can awake as a forgiven creature in God's eyes that I'm able to plunge into the struggle with Paul and say with him, "Not that I have already obtained all this, or have already been made perfect, but I press on to take hold of that for which Christ Jesus took hold of me. Brothers, I do not consider myself yet to have taken hold of it. But one thing I do: Forgetting what is behind and straining toward what is ahead, I press on toward the goal to win the prize for which God has called me heavenward in Christ Jesus" (Philippians 3:12-14, NIV).

And I cannot help closing with these words of Paul which follow after that. "All of us who are mature should take such a view of things. And if on some point you think differently, that too God will make clear to you. Only let us live up to what we have already attained" (Philippians 3:15, 16, NIV).

Only let us live up to what we have already attained.

13
TRUE WISDOM IS HEAVENLY

Is there some wise and understanding man among you? Then let his life be a shining example of the humility that is born of true wisdom. But if your heart is full of bitter jealousy and rivalry, then do not boast and do not deny the truth. You may acquire a certain wisdom, but it does not come from above—it comes from this world, from your own lower nature, even from the devil. For wherever you find jealousy and rivalry you also find disharmony and all other kinds of evil. The wisdom that comes from above is first pure, then peace-loving, gentle, approachable, full of merciful thoughts and kindly actions, straightforward, with no hint of hypocrisy. And the peacemakers go on quietly sowing for a harvest of righteousness (James 3:13-18).

Ambition is as American as apple pie. Who hasn't hoped (out loud) that their son will be ambitious about what he wants to be? "Think big!" has been with us for a long time. Being humble is okay in the abstract, but not many of us go around telling our friends what a humble son or daughter we have.

Is there some wise and understanding man among you? Then let his life be a shining example of the humility that is born of true wisdom.

Tension: Can a man be ambitious and not be selfish?

A Closer Look at Ambition

The Bible is full of men and women who had great ambitions. Abraham was ambitious. Joshua was ambitious. David was ambitious. And although they were sinful men, were they not men with whom God was pleased? The New International Version translates James 3:14 (and 3:16) "bitter envy and *selfish* ambition." Evidently it is a matter of motivation.

Ambition for what?

Western men and women are future oriented. Our lives are controlled by our future goals. We are motivated to achieve what we consider to be desirable goals. Abraham Maslow[1] has pointed out to us that we can picture ourselves as having a hierarchy of goals and motivations. At the bottom of the hierarchy are the most basic needs of food and drink. If we are hungry, if we are thirsty, then these will become our immediate and primary goals. All of our motivation will be in the direction of meeting our hunger and thirst needs. We will put aside thoughts of personal safety to accept very high risk in order to meet these needs.

But once our hunger and thirst needs are met, we then become concerned with the next level of need which is the need, or goal, for safety. If we feel that our hunger and thirst and safety needs are met, then we move on to setting goals for meeting our needs for love and sexual satisfaction.

Next up on Maslow's hierarchy are needs for self-esteem, to be respected, to be thought of as people who are righteous, people who do good.

Maslow caps his hierarchy with what he calls "self-actualization." Maslow was not a Christian. Self-actualization is as close as he came. For the Christian this might be thought of as resting completely in Christ, for it is only as we are completely in Him that we find our true humanity.

All of this helps us to see that ambition has to do with goals, things that we want to see happen some time in the future.[2]

James keeps coming back to pride and selfish ambition as being avoided at all costs. What is the antidote to misdirected ambition?

Antidote to Misdirected Ambition

Interestingly, James sets over and against ambition "wisdom from above."

Phillips translates it as "pure, then peace-loving, gentle, approachable, full of merciful thoughts and kindly actions, straightforward, with no hint of hypocrisy" (3:17).

But is this practical? Can one live in the world like that? For example, could you be a successful businessman? Let's make a list of James's statements about wisdom from above and list them against how you might act in business.

Wisdom from Above	Business Action
Pure	Clear motivation
Peaceable	Not manipulative
Gentle	Not taking position advantage
Approachable, full of merciful thoughts and kindly actions	Ready to accept mistakes
Without hint of hypocrisy	Not saying one thing and doing another

Surprisingly, this is exactly what many of the modern management theorists are telling us as to how we should relate within business life. Their rationale is not that it will make us better people, or that we will feel better about ourselves, but rather that it is *good business!*[3]

In contrast, what happens when "selfish ambition" gets into our relationships, say a marriage? Each individual says, "I want to be":

He Says	She Says
"I want to be . . ."	**"I want to be . . ."**
"Me!"	"Me!"
"Loved"	"Loved"
"Appreciated"	"Appreciated"
"A good father"	"A good mother"
"Sexually competent"	"Sexually competent"
"Professionally successful"	"Professionally successful"
"Right"	"Right"

Both are saying the same thing, of course; both are focusing their ambition upon themselves rather than upon the marriage. How different the marriage could be if we applied this "wisdom from above."[4]

"Rivalry and bitter jealousy" are the result or the root of selfish ambition. The Bible tells us that I may become good at what I am doing, and may even boast about it, but success that is based on selfish ambition is the result of the "below," not the "above." (And somehow in my heart I know this.)

> "For whoever would save his life will lose it, and who-
> ever loses his life for my sake will find it"—Jesus
> (Matthew 16:25, RSV).

One of my favorite figures of history is St. Augustine. For me his most memorable comment on how we should live was, "Love God and do as you please!" St. Augustine's assumption was that as I attempt to love the Lord with all my soul, strength, heart, and mind, then what I do will please Him. Now, I never expect that I will love God that thoroughly in this earthly life. But there is a direction there, a pointing toward the way I should go, that gives me a reason to be ambitious, ambitious to love God. Is there some way I can *know* if I love him?

People sometimes ask me if I pray out the decisions I make. I usually respond, "Not usually." "Then how," they ask, "do you know if you are doing God's will?" It is then that I quote St. Augustine and go on to quote Jesus' words of John 13:35. The way I can know the quality of my love for God is by the quality of my love for my brothers and sisters in Christ. The answer, then, to good decisions and right ambition is love toward my brothers.

The Goals of God

God has put into men a desire to *become*, to change the world in which they live.

But in the midst of this striving to be God's men and women, there are two dangers. The first is that as we become "successful," we will turn from honoring God to honoring ourselves. John Wesley decried the fact that when men became religious they became industrious, and when they became industrious they became wealthy— and when they became wealthy they became irreligious!

In his *Pedagogy of the Oppressed*, Paulo Friere points out the natural inclination of the poor to become oppressors themselves when *they* become rich. The question is, why do we want to succeed? Certainly there is that built-in ambition in us to change things. But we need to go beyond that.

Most of us have heard the story of the young man who was being questioned by his father, "What will you do next, my son?"

"Well, I plan to graduate from college."

"And then what will you do?"

"Well, I suppose I will get a job and get married."

"And then what will happen after that?"

"I want to have children. I want to be successful in business."

"And then?"

"Well, I suppose I will grow older and retire."

"And after that?"

"I guess I will die."

"And then . . . ?"

Years ago there was a little chorus entitled "With Eternity's Values in View." That's what it's all about, isn't it? Eternity's values. Eternity's values have to do with people and relationships. When our goals are turned from survival to love and ultimately the ultimate love of Christ, then the danger of turning from God is much reduced.

The second danger is that the accomplishments will become ends in themselves. We can so easily lose sight of our primary purpose.

The antidote is the same as for the success problem. We need to connect up accomplishments into making God's will what we believe He would have it to be.

Wisdom calls us to keep striving and not be content with success. Move on! to "give glory to God and enjoy Him forever."

Notes

1. Abraham Maslow, *Motivation and Personality*.

2. Goals have tremendous power to motivate us. Ted Engstrom and I have tried to utilize this fact in a Christian context. See *Strategy for Living*.

3. The list of references is endless. Rensis Likert has already been mentioned. Others would include Harry Levinson, *The Exceptional Executive;* Douglas McGregor, *The Human Side of Organization;* and *Professional Manager.* More recently theorists are trying to explain how the Japanese approach of giving equal priority to the task and the people can be worked out.

4. I cannot help making a brief foray into the ongoing discussion about "submission" of the wife in marriage. Wisdom from above sees the Ephesians 5 passage as focusing on first submission to one another, but emphasizes the submission of love demanded of the husband, the kind of "servant" love Christ had for the church.

14
I GAVE HIM MY LIFE, BUT I WANT IT BACK

But what about the feuds and struggles that exist among you—where do you suppose they come from? Can't you see that they arise from conflicting desires for pleasure within yourselves? You crave for something and don't get it; you are murderously jealous of what you can't possess yourselves; you struggle and fight with one another. You don't get what you want because you don't ask God for it. And when you do ask he doesn't give it to you, for you ask in quite the wrong spirit—you only want to satisfy your own desires.

You are like unfaithful wives, never realising that to be the world's lover means becoming the enemy of God! Anyone who chooses to be the world's friend is thereby making himself God's enemy. Or do you think what the scriptures have to say about this is a mere formality? Do you imagine that this spirit of passionate jealousy is the Spirit he has caused to live in us? Yet he gives us grace which is stronger. That is why he says:

> God resisteth the proud,
> But giveth grace to the humble.

Be humble then before God. But resist the devil and you'll find he'll run away from you. Come close to God and he will come close to you. You are sinners: get your hands clean again. Your loyalty is divided: get your

hearts made true once more. You should be deeply sorry,
you should be grieved, you should even be in tears. Your
laughter will have become mourning, your high spirits
will have to become dejection. You must humble yourselves in the sight of the Lord before he will lift you up
(James 4:1-10).

All of James seems to center around the warfare that goes on
within the Christian, the battle to take back what has been given
over to the Spirit of God. How nice it would be if once we had turned
over our lives to the Savior, that was all there was to it. I suspect that
the whole world would be Christian by now!

But it isn't like that.

A Continual Tug of War

A "commmitment to Christ" is a beginning, not an ending. There
is a battle to be waged, a battle so fierce that Paul describes it as a
"warfare."

The Bible is consistent in picturing the Christian life this way.
James, Peter, and Paul all speak in similar terms. "I am speaking in
human terms, because of your natural limitations. . . . yield your
members to righteousness for sanctification" (Romans 6:19, RSV).

There is a continual tug of war going on. Two powerful forces are
competing for our attention. The "world" is noisy and seductive and
ever putting on a new disguise. It is ruled by a master theatrical pro-
ducer—Satan. Each day it seems to offer a new variety of entice-
ments.

The life in the Spirit is open and transparent, and therefore all-
too-familiar. Why, it's almost dull. If we have been brought up in a
Christian home, nurtured in a Sunday school, and attended a
church much of our life, it is easy to develop a feeling that we have
experienced all that the life called Christian has to offer. That which
was perhaps once so exciting has now become everyday routine. We
begin to compare ourselves with other Christians and find that we
are really doing quite well. Perhaps in our more realistic moments
we realize that we are no longer living the life that is Christian. But
we somehow think it is always available, and "soon" we will get
around to living it.

And so we become like unfaithful wives (or husbands) who long
for the enrichment of a new liaison without recognizing how it will
destroy our marriage to Christ.[1] Perhaps you had never thought
about it that way. Let's paraphrase James for a moment: "You are

like unfaithful wives, flirting with the glamour of another man and never realizing that to be someone else's lover means becoming the enemy of your husband. Anyone who deliberately chooses to love another man is thereby making herself her husband's enemy."[2]

My wife, Marge, is a professional marriage and family counselor. She often says that it's not so much a matter of having to work at a marriage as it is to make time for it. One of the things that so easily happens to us as older Christians is that we no longer make the time. The very familiarity of what we have done in the past dulls our desire to spend time with others in worship and prayer, to serve as members of Christ's body. Our enthusiasm seems to be gone.

We are faced with a matter of our *will*. God has still left us in charge. Why He was pleased to do this is not for us to say. God is God. The question is, will we align our will for Him or against Him?

God's Spirit or My Spirit?

Assuming that God's Spirit "has been made to dwell in us," what can we will to do that will move us toward the Spirit? If we are really walking away, how do we turn back? James starts by telling us to "submit yourselves to God" (4:7), and then gives us four steps to take.

1. *Resist the devil* (4:7).

Peter tells us the same thing (1 Peter 5:8, 9). Paul expresses it in Ephesians 4:27. "Give no opportunity for the devil." How to do that? Recognize that he is the source of evil. Realize that the "power (God's Spirit) that is in you is greater than the power that is in the world." "He (the devil) will flee from you."

It is interesting that we don't have to pursue him, just stand firm against him and the powers of darkness.

> Finally, be strong in the Lord and in his mighty power. Put on the full armor of God so that you can take your stand against the devil's schemes. For our struggle is not against flesh and blood, but against the rulers, against the authorities, against the powers of this dark world and against the spiritual forces of evil in the heavenly realms. Therefore put on the full armor of God, so that when the day of evil comes, you may be able to stand your ground, and after you have done everything, to stand. Stand firm then, with the belt of truth buckled around your waist, with the breastplace of righteousness in place, and with your feet fitted with the readiness that comes from the

gospel of peace. In addition to all this, take up the shield of faith, with which you can extinguish all the flaming arrows of the evil one. Take the helmet of salvation and the sword of the Spirit, which is the word of God. And pray in the Spirit on all occasions with all kinds of prayers and requests. With this in mind, be alert and always keep on praying for all the saints (Ephesians 6:10-18, NIV).

2. *Come close to God* (4:8). How strange it is that we forget that He is a person, and we can draw *away* from Him. We draw near to God when we acknowledge Him just as we would acknowledge another person.

As human beings we can only show ourselves in human ways. God's response is assured. As we come close to Him, so He draws near to us.

How quickly we forget that God is willing and pleased to deal with us in our humanity. In many ways He asks nothing more than that we deal with Him as we would deal with the best of all our friends or relatives.

Do you have dates in your appointment book when you will draw near to Him? Rebuilding love often takes time, particularly when indifference has separated us. Perhaps the Holy Spirit will overcome us with a new and fresh affection. More often we need to consciously plan to be with the Lord.

Do you extend Him the same courtesy that you would extend to a fellow employee as you walk down the hall and acknowledge His greeting? Do you plan for and look forward to time with Him?

3. *Get your hands clean again* (4:8).

I suppose that girls get dirty, too, but I've noticed that when our son was young, he and his friends seemed to attract dirt and grime as a magnet attracts iron filings. After they made one or two trips in and out of the house, one could follow their trail by the handmarks along the doorjambs and on the doorknobs.

Our sins are very much like that. They make us dirty. As we move through life, they mark up everything that is around us. What a blessed thought is that word from 1 John: "If we confess our sins, he is faithful and just and will forgive us our sins and purify us from all unrighteousness" (1 John 1:9, NIV).

It's not easy—

As you come close to God you should be deeply sorry, you should be grieved, you should even be in tears. Your life will have to become mourning, your high spirits will have to become heartfelt dejection. You will have to feel very small in the sight of God before He will set you on your feet once more.

Confess our sins to *one another?* It's not easy, as we'll discuss later, but it can be very effective in "cleaning us up."

James calls God "the Father of all lights." The closer we are to God, the more evident our sins become! Perhaps we thought we were all cleaned up. Perhaps we thought we had learned everything about ourselves there was to learn. But as we walk through life with Him, the glory and intensity of His presence keeps breaking through the shutters that have secured so many areas of our life. New understanding brings new requirements to cleanse away the encrusted dirt of former years. It needs to be acknowledged and confessed, not only to God but to one another.

4. *Get your hearts made true once more* (4:8).

This is aimed at the double-minded man of 1:8. A pure heart is one that is undivided. Make up your mind! Is it going to be God or a no-God?

The prophet Elijah said it so well. In 1 Kings 18 we read of the contest that he had with the priests of Baal over who was to rule Israel: "So Ahab sent to all the people of Israel, and gathered the prophets together at Mount Carmel. And Elijah came near to all the people, and said, 'How long will you go limping with two different opinions? If the LORD is God, follow him, but if Baal, then follow him '" (1 Kings 18:20-21a, RSV).

How long will you go limping with two different opinions? It's as though we were walking along a curb with one foot in the gutter and one on the sidewalk. What a ludicrous sight!

What will it be? God's Spirit or my spirit?

The paradox remains. God is completely sovereign, and yet He has given me freedom to act.

The tension is continuous. There is a warfare to be waged, a battle to be fought. But a faith that goes further conquers all things. Thanks be to God who gives us the victory in Jesus Christ!

Notes

1. Is it possible to fall completely from grace? Is it possible to "lose" our salvation? The Christian Church has been divided over this for 1900 years. I must admit that I never seem to come out completely on one side of the issue or the other any more. Some days I am a Calvinist Arminian and other days I'm an Arminian Calvinist. But certainly passages such as Hebrews

6:4-8 should give us enough pause to stop taking our salvation for granted. In any event, it is obvious that in this life we, even as Christians, can displease our Lord. Even the thought of that seems unbelievable and yet experience tells us that it is true.

2. Verse 5 could be alternately translated, "or do you think Scripture says without reason that spirit He caused to live within us tends toward envy," or it could be translated, "or that God jealously longs for the spirit that he made to live within us." I have rather arbitrarily followed Phillips.

15
GOD'S PURPOSE VERSUS PEOPLE'S PLANS

Just a moment, now, you who say, "We are going to such-and-such a city today or tomorrow. We shall stay there a year doing business and make a profit"! How do you know what will happen tomorrow? What, after all, is your life? It is like a puff of smoke visible for a little while and then dissolving into thin air. Your remarks should be prefaced with, "If it is the Lord's will, we shall still be alive and will do so-and-so." As it is, you take a certain pride in planning with such confidence. That sort of pride is all wrong. No doubt you agree with the above in theory.

Well, then, if a man knows what is right and fails to do it, his failure is a real sin (James 4:13-17).

If planners are born and not made (which I doubt!), then I was born a planner. I *like* to plan! I like to think about what might happen tomorrow, how the future might be better. It's exciting to dream dreams and see them shape into reality.

I believe in the power of goals, the idea of deciding what it is God wants you to be or to do and working toward that.[1] In a society which is continually drawing its net tighter and tighter around us and seeking to have us conform to the mandates of a technological humanism, I *want* to imagine how my family, my church, and my organizations could take steps that would make us be different, more honoring to God.

> Just a moment, now, you who say, "We are going to such-and-such a city today or tomorrow. We shall stay there a year doing business and make a profit"! How do you know what will happen tomorrow?

Is James speaking specifically to planners like me?

Our Freedom Versus God's Control

This is probably the best illustration of the biblical relationship between our freedom to be ourselves and God's sovereignty. Let's explore that a moment. What do we mean by God's sovereignty?

One might think of God's sovereignty like the air that we breathe. It is all around us. We are usually completely unconscious of its presence. We can do whatever we like, whenever we like, yet we are always dependent on the air we breathe. We are in His context, His environment. We don't have to look very far through the Bible to find examples of the Lord's sovereignty.

> Whatever the Lord pleases he does, in heaven and on earth, in the seas and all deeps (Psalm 135:6, RSV).

> All the inhabitants of the earth are accounted as nothing; and he does according to his will in the host of heaven and among the inhabitants of the earth (Daniel 4:35, RSV).

> For we are God's workmanship, created in Christ Jesus to do good works, which God prepared in advance for us to do (Ephesians 2:10, NIV).

God has prepared all of the good works that we're going to do in advance. God's sovereignty for the Christian says that we do nothing that God has not thought about ahead of time.

Are we then not to plan? Is it a sin to set goals? At first glance, this text might seem like a brief against planning, but it is not. What is wrong, as Phillips translates it, "is you take a certain pride in planning with such confidence. *That* sort of pride is all wrong."

James gives us example after example of Christians who want to take their life into their own hands.

James 1:5-8	He warns us against double-mindedness.
James 1:9-11	He warns us against dependence on wealth.
James 1:12-15	He demands we be responsible for our own sin.
James 1:19-21, 1:26-27, 3:1-12	He points out the danger of an uncontrolled tongue.

94

James 1:22-24, 2:14-16	He shows the uselessness of depending on a faith that does not produce fruit.
James 2:1-13	He deplores a Christianity that shows partiality, that somehow assumes one person is more important than another.
James 3:13-18	He points out the danger of selfish ambition.
James 4:1-12	He asks us to reject the world system and concentrate on God's system.

Don't try to take your life into your own hands! Remember that all you do is dependent upon God's good will.

If you read letters between Christians one hundred or more years ago, very often you will find after a sentence the letters "D.V." D.V. stands for *Deo volente*, Latin for "if God wills," or "God willing."

Puffs of Smoke and Plans for Action

All plans, all goals should be made as *statements of faith*. Any statement about tomorrow is a statement of faith:

How do you know what will happen tomorrow? What, after all, is your life? It is like a puff of smoke visible for a little while and then dissolving into thin air.

But here is the paradox: the responsibility always rests with us! No more complete statement of the paradox could be made than the one that Jesus made in Luke 22:22 as He spoke of His forthcoming death: "The Son of Man will go as it has been decreed, but woe to that man who betrays him" (Luke 22:22, NIV).

We are responsible. Christianity does not picture humankind as caught up in a great stream of life, unable to do anything but drift through the current. Christ does not ask us to completely lose our personality or to become a mere molecule in the larger mass.

It boggles the mind, but it does not have to destroy one's faith. Jesus calls upon us to live in complete dependence upon Him. Jesus calls upon us to make plans for tomorrow, to stretch out to reach the goal of righteousness, justice, goodness—all those things which we know are His good will for us and the rest of the world.

Now we come to the everyday business of living—not the question of whether what we are doing is right or wrong, but the question of the attitude with which we do it.

As it is, you take a certain pride in planning with such confidence. That sort of pride is all wrong.

James then nails the attitude question down by pointing out: "No

95

doubt you agree with the above in theory. Well then, if a man knows what is right and fails to do it, his failure is a real sin."

To not accept the paradox is sin! There is a responsibility that comes with knowledge.

But even as our knowledge increases, we realize more and more the need for the mature Christian to live the life of faith in the midst of ambiguity and paradox. I cannot possibly understand how it is that God is completely sovereign, that all I do is by His permissive will, and yet at the same time understand how I am in control and *responsible* for my actions. I believe it because the revealed Word of God tells me that it is so, and that this is the nature of the creation. Then as I act on what I believe, I discover that it works.

Accusing the Maker of Creating Evil

There is another side to this paradox between God's purpose and our plans that needs to be explored. How easy it is when something happens to us to thank or blame God. Some bad thing happens to us, and we so easily say, "Well, the Lord knew that I needed that. . . . "

"No!" says James. "You can't say that."

> Let no one say when he is tempted, "I am tempted by God"; for God cannot be tempted with evil and he himself tempts no one (James 1:13, RSV).

Evil may befall us. It may be of our own making. It may be the product of our society with its sinful men. It may be the result of the work of Satan. But it is not the work of God.

And yet God will get glory from it. And not only that, but ultimately He will work it together for good. Joseph's brothers had sold him into slavery in Egypt. There he had become second only to the Pharaoh in his authority. But when Joseph eventually confronted his brothers in Egypt, they were certain he would put them to death. Instead he said, "You meant evil against me; but God meant it for good" (Genesis 50:20, RSV). What they did was evil. They were responsible for that evil. The fact that God turned it into good doesn't change either the evil or the responsibility.

If we don't accept this paradox, this mystery hidden from us, then ultimately we will accuse God of creating the evil of the universe. Again, let me take you back to Paul and Romans 9: "You will say to me then, 'Why does he still find fault? For who can resist his will?' " (v. 19, RSV).

Paul doesn't answer the question. He just points us back to the Creator: "But who are you, a man, to answer back to God? Will what is molded say to its molder, 'Why have you made me thus?' " (Romans 9:20, RSV).

The life of faith is one lived in constant recognition that, as Paul told his Athenian audience on Mars Hill (Acts 17:28, RSV), " 'In him we live and move and have our being.' "

Think you are in control? "All such boasting is evil." And once you know that and fail to live in dependence, it is *sin*.

A verse that meant much to me and perhaps sums it up well is Proverbs 16:9. The Revised Standard Version translates it, "A man's mind plans his way, but the LORD directs his steps."

Notes
___

1. Ted Engstrom and I elaborate on this in our books *Strategy for Living* and *Strategy for Leadership*. I have dealt with the how-to of goal setting and planning in *God's Purpose/Man's Plans*.

16
PATIENCE LIVES ON EXPECTATION

But be patient, my brothers, as you wait for the Lord to come. Look at the farmer quietly awaiting the precious harvest of his hand. See how he has to possess his soul in patience till the early and late rains have fallen. So must you be patient, resting your hearts on the ultimate certainty. The Lord's coming is very near.

Don't make complaints against each other in the meantime, my brothers—you may be the one at fault yourself. The judge himself is already at the door.

For our example of the patient endurance of suffering we can take the prophets who have spoken in the Lord's name. Remember that it is those who have patiently endured to whom we accord the word "blessed". You have heard of Job's patient endurance and how the Lord dealt with him in the end, and therefore you have seen that the Lord is merciful and full of understanding pity (James 5:7-11).

We are living in a day when there is a great deal of discussion and anticipation about the return of the Lord. We are confident that He is coming again. It need not concern us here whether we believe or do not believe in a particular interpretation of the events that will surround His coming and the establishing of His kingdom. The Bible assures us that the "blessed hope" that we have is that all things do work together for good for those who love the Lord and look forward to His coming. The hope is that one day we will be made whole persons, we will feel ourselves to be complete—physically, emotionally, spiritually.

Christians have a straight-line view of history. We do not picture ourselves going through a cycle of reincarnation with one life dissolving into another, into another, and on into eternity. Rather, we look forward to the culmination of history, to a time when evil will be put aside. We will consciously dwell in God's presence.

Why Is Christ's Coming Important?

Why is Christ's coming so important? Wouldn't it just be all right if when we died all who believed went to be with the Lord? Why does He have to come *again*?

The answer lies in God's concern for His whole creation. We are living in a "fallen" world, and the Bible says that God intends not only to redeem men but to redeem the entire system for which He created them. The world was created for man, and God intends one day to restore things to the way they were meant to be.

> But in keeping with his promise we are looking forward to a new heaven and a new earth, the home of righteousness (2 Peter 3:13, NIV).

I like the way Phillips translates Romans 8:18-21.

> In my opinion whatever we may have to go through now is less than nothing compared with the magnificent future God has in store for us. The whole creation is on tiptoe to see the wonderful sight of the sons of God coming into their own. The world of creation cannot as yet see reality, not because it chooses to be blind, but because in God's purpose it has been so limited—yet it has been given hope. And the hope is that in the end the whole of created life will be rescued from the tyranny of change and decay, and have its share in that magnificent liberty which can only belong to the children of God!

Christ's coming is important also because it has a finality and completeness about it. It will be a visual demonstration to all the world that He is God, and He will do according to His pleasure.

Facing the Difficulties with Patience

The New Testament writers emphasize the coming of the Lord because they face up to the difficulty of life. But even as they tell us to hold firmly to that hope, they caution us to *be* the kind of people with whom God will be pleased when Christ comes, and to be *doing* those things that please Him until He comes.

God's Spirit says to us: Be patient, endure, my child. Christ is coming, and He will make it all right. "Therefore lift your drooping hands and strengthen your weak knees, and make straight paths for your feet, so that what is lame may not be put out of joint but rather be healed" (Hebrews 12:12, 13, RSV. See what follows also.)

But our own spirit says back, "Where is the promise of his coming? For ever since the fathers fell asleep, all things have continued as they were from the beginning of creation" (2 Peter 3:4, RSV). I am weary of enduring. It is much easier to give in and take back control of my life. I'm tired of these Christians I associate with. They are often a sorry lot. This one is always preaching at me, and that one certainly is living a miserable life. What's the point?

In reply James tells us to remember the prophets and especially Job. We know all about Job. We have read God's Word. We have had the opportunity to push aside the curtain of history and see what Job could not see, what was really going on behind the scenes.[1] We are assured that all the time Job was suffering the attacks of Satan that God was very much in control of his life. James tells us history calls men like Job blessed, and so do we (James 5:11).

In Hebrews 11, the writer gives example after example of all kinds of people who held on in faith and then goes on to tell us: "Therefore, since we are surrounded by so great a cloud of witnesses, let us also lay aside every weight, and sin which clings so closely, and let us run with perseverance the race that is set before us, looking to Jesus the pioneer [He's been there before us!] and perfecter of our faith . . ." (Hebrews 12:1, 2, RSV).

Patience versus expectation.

Living in Expectation . . . Unexpectantly

Patience can lead to resignation and living in the status quo. Expectation can get us so excited about what might happen tomorrow that we neglect to be about the Lord's business today.

We should be excited about the Lord's coming. He will come!

Our entire expectation is that the Lord will come. But even though the biblical writers felt the "Lord's coming is very near" (James 5:8), they looked upon this as a fact in whose light they should live, rather than something that they should take into their planning.[2] Paul tells us, "But you are not in darkness, brethren, for that day to surprise you like a thief. For you are all sons of light . . ." (1 Thessalonians 5:4-5, RSV).

We need to live in the *unexpectedness* of His coming, practicing the presence of Christ in our daily routine and thought life.

Jesus will come like a thief for those who are in darkness. Such people are surprised that He will come to judge (James 5:9). "But of that day and hour no one knows, not even the angels of heaven, nor the Son, but the Father only" (Matthew 24:36, RSV). "Therefore you also must be ready; for the Son of Man is coming at an hour you do not expect" (Matthew 24:44, RSV). Jesus then goes on to give illustrations of those who act as though the Master was not going to return for some time.

The judge himself is already at the door (James 5:9).

How would we act if at any moment we knew the door of our office or home might open and a judge would approve or condemn what we had just said or done? Picture yourself having a business discussion in your office, trying to decide whether this was the right or wrong approach to a problem. How would your discussion or decision be affected if you knew the moment after you had made it the door would open and Jesus would walk in to evaluate your discussion? Or imagine you are having a cup of coffee with a friend and discussing a situation at church, a problem that involved personality differences. How might your conversation be different?

> The end of all things is near. Therefore be clear minded and self-controlled so that you can pray. Above all, love each other deeply because love covers over a multitude of sins. Offer hospitality to one another without grumbling. Each one should use whatever gift he has received to serve others, faithfully administering God's grace in its various forms. If anyone speaks, he should do it as one speaking the very words of God. If anyone serves, he should do it with the strength God provides, so that in all things God may be praised through Jesus Christ. To him be the glory and the power forever and ever. Amen (1 Peter 4:7-11, NIV).

There is a reason Jesus has not come yet.

> Do not forget this one thing, dear friends: With the Lord a day is like a thousand years, and a thousand years are like a day. The Lord is not slow in keeping his promise, as some understand slowness. He is patient with you, not

wanting anyone to perish, but everyone to come to repentance (2 Peter 3:8, 9, NIV).

Paradox. Tension? Live in faith.

Notes

1. Job 1, 2.

2. For a good insight into this, reread Matthew 24 and 25. The disciples wanted to know about the details of Christ's coming. He wanted them to understand how they should live in light of the fact that He would indeed come again.

17
WHEN DO I NEED
A DOCTOR?

If any of you is in trouble let him pray. If anyone is flourishing let him sing praises to God. If anyone is ill he should send for the church elders. They should pray over him, anointing him with oil in the Lord's name. Believing prayer will save the sick man; the Lord will restore him and any sins that he has committed will be forgiven. You should get into the habit of admitting your sins to each other, and praying for each other, so that you may be healed (James 5:13-16a).

There are two sets of contrasts in these verses and the verses which follow. They are so interwoven that we will deal with them in two chapters.

A Spiritual Illness or a Physical Illness?

Let's begin with spiritual versus physical. This contrast is wrapped up in such questions as, should we go to a doctor when we are ill, or should we perhaps just ask for prayer? Is illness all caused by external forces loose in the world—bacteria, viruses—or is it all due to sin? How should the Christian look upon the relationship between what's going on in the physical person and what's going on inside the spiritual person? Or is it really a question of either/or?

Although writers of the New Testament at times use Greek thought in describing the various manifestations of mankind (". . . spirit and soul and body"—1 Thessalonians 5:23, RSV), their overall view is more the Hebrew one of wholeness. We cannot be understood as separate, unrelated parts. Words such as *physical, spiritual, psychological, emotional* are all categories which we use to describe what's going on within us.

None of us has to be told how complex we are and how mysterious is the makeup of the human being. For example, how many "persons" are we really? How is it possible that I can think about myself thinking about something? I can stand outside myself and watch "myself" have a conversation. We talk about (as does the Bible) "my spirit is troubled" when we mean that we emotionally are not satisfied with that condition. We say, "I'm ill," when we mean that we are physically ill at ease. Or we may say, "I'm upset!" What part of the "I" is not right with the world?

Unfortunately, too often we have neatly divided ourselves up into categories of "spiritual" and "physical." And though we (Western) Christians have accepted the idea that when our "physical" person is not as it should be, we should seek the counsel of a medical doctor, we often assume that anything that is not physical must be "spiritual"; and therefore we need to seek the counsel of a spiritual doctor.

But we are just not that simple, are we? Slowly we are beginning to see that just as there are specialties in physical medicine, so there are specialties in these other dimensions of our lives. Many times we need the counsel of a psychologist, a "doctor of the emotions," if you will.

Most of us are not too happy with this idea. It is really quite convenient to divide the person up between the spiritual and the physical. It is certainly much easier to give advice to others when we can separate the two!

The tension comes from trying to understand whether what we're facing requires "spiritual" healing or "emotional" healing. To make matters worse, we are now beginning to understand that physical illness may be a result of "emotional" illness or "spiritual" illness.

Isn't it surprising that we are "discovering" something which the Bible has talked about all along?

There is an obvious connection between *unconfessed* sin and physical well-being. The Psalmist put it this way: "When I declared not my sin, my body wasted away through my groaning all day long" (Psalm 32:3, RSV).

To experience that, all we have to do is to remember sometime when we were frightened of being caught doing something wrong. "Fright" is not just something that happens inside. We begin to perspire and maybe even to tremble. The throat constricts. We feel unable to move. Which "person" is doing which?

That there is a relationship between some illness and sin is illustrated many times in the Bible. Jesus said to the paralytic in Mark 2:5 (RSV), "My son, your sins are forgiven" and explained in Mark 2:9 that sin is harder to cleanse than illness. But there is not a *necessary* connection. Read Jesus' reply to His disciples when asked the question about the blind man: "Rabbi, who sinned, this man or his parents . . . ?" (John 9:2, RSV). Jesus' reply was, "It was not that this man sinned, or his parents, but that the works of God might be made manifest in him."

Confession, Transparency, Sin, and the Soul

But confessing sin to God is not enough. We need to confess our sins to one another.

> You should get into the habit of admitting your sins to each other, and praying for each other, so that you may be healed.

The secular psychologist Mowrer[1] makes the interesting observation that early Christians really understood the basis of psychological help: Being open and transparent to one another was the road to emotional maturity. He goes on to point out that the Roman church took away part of this emotional cleansing by saying that we only had to confess our sins to the priest. The Protestants took it a step further by saying we only had to confess our sins to God. Finally, Freud completely ruined the whole thing by denying that we had any sin to confess!

> Confess your sins to one another.

This is part of the transparent life that is Christian. We are made righteous as we have faith and then as we confess our sin. "If we confess our sins, he is faithful and just, and will forgive our sins and cleanse us from all unrighteousness" (1 John 1:9, RSV). As we hold back from one another, our prayers are held back. (Peter tells us that lack of consideration in a marriage really hinders prayer [1 Peter 3:7].)

But we don't like to confess our sins to one another, do we? Once we open ourselves to another person and confess our shortcomings, we give another person power over us. (Do you remember playing the game "I'll tell you a secret about me, if you'll tell me a secret about you" when you were young?) There is great responsibility in accepting another's confession of sin. There is a responsibility *not* to exercise the power that it gives us.

> Brothers, if someone is caught in a sin, you who are spiritual should restore him gently. But watch yourself, or you also may be tempted. Carry each other's burdens, and in this way you will fulfill the law of Christ. If anyone thinks he is something when he is nothing, he deceives himself. Each one should test his own actions. Then he can take pride in himself, without comparing himself to somebody else, for each one should carry his own load (Galatians 6:1-5, NIV).

The more I understand about myself, the more difficult I become to understand! What's the answer? How do we handle this unknown relationship between the physical and spiritual? James gives us some concepts that will form a good bridge into the next chapter.

A Secret for the Physical/Spiritual Dilemma

First, always live in recognition of our continuing relationship to God. "If any of you is in trouble let him pray. If anyone is flourishing let him sing praises to God."

Paul claimed in Philippians 4:12 that he had learned a secret: "I know how to be abased, and I know how to abound; in any and all circumstances I have learned the secret of facing plenty and hunger, abundance and want" (RSV).

What was the secret? "I can do all things in him who strengthens me" (Philippians 4:13, RSV). Or as Phillips translates it: "I am ready for anything through the strength of the One who lives within me."

Second, live within relationship, within the church: "If anyone is ill he should send for the church elders."

It may be that we are completely unable to pray to God. It is at times like these we need one another.

Third, be transparent with one another. "You should get into the habit of admitting your sins to each other and praying for one another, so that you may be healed."

Let us have done with masks and role playing. Let us see each other as God sees us: new creations in Christ (2 Corinthians 5:17).

Notes

1. See O. Hobart Mowrer, *The New Group Therapy*.

18
WHEN IS IT TIME
TO PRAY?

If any of you is in trouble let him pray. If anyone is flourishing let him sing praises to God. If anyone is ill he should send for the church elders. They should pray over him, anointing him with oil in the Lord's name. Believing prayer will save the sick man; the Lord will restore him and any sins that he has committed will be forgiven. You should get into the habit of admitting your sins to each other, and praying for each other, so that you may be healed.

Tremendous power is made available through a good man's earnest prayer. Do you remember Elijah? He was a man as human as we are but he prayed earnestly that it should not rain. In fact, not a drop fell on the land for three and a half years. Then he prayed again, the heavens gave the rain and the earth sprouted with vegetation again (James 5:13-18).

When should we pray, and when should we "act"?[1]

Some time ago I listened as a young man explained about how the place of prayer was a resting place for him after the battle of living. I wish I could say the same. Prayer for me is where the struggle really is.

I find prayer to be work! I have to continually struggle to pray. For the past few years I have been writing my prayers in a blank book, not so much that I may go back and read what I have said, but rather just to make sure that I am praying. Perhaps you don't go through this struggle.

Sometimes I like to hide behind the excuse that those of us who are Christian "professionals," who are finding our livelihood by being involved in missions and Christian teaching, are really "praying" all the time. After all, doesn't the Lord hear all of our conversations? And yet I know in my heart that prayer is *consciously* bringing myself as a person into God's presence as a Person.

But I like the way James starts this section: "If any of you is in trouble let him pray. If anyone is flourishing let him sing praises to God."

For sometimes I feel guilty about only praying when I'm in trouble, and I forget that singing praises to God is a form of prayer also.

What Is Prayer?

First and foremost, prayer is consciously addressing God, recognizing that we are in His presence and remembering that our highest human conception of Him is a Person.

Second, prayer is therefore a matter of the will.[2] We choose to pray or not to pray. God has given us freedom to do as we please.

Third, it is a matter of attitude. James warns us about being "double-minded" in our prayer (1:8, 4:9). Don't use "God willing" as a cop-out. (See chapter 5.) Believe God will answer. This is a very difficult task for most of us. Yet we are called upon to pray for what we know (believe) in our hearts is right and not to be discouraged or turned aside when we do not receive "answers" of the kind we contemplated. This takes maturity. (If God answered the prayers of every Christian all over the world in the way that each individual thought best, the world wouldn't work too well!)

This is a mystery, and a difficult one. But we see that the Apostle Paul faced the same thing. Here was a man who was able to do all kinds of acts for God through prayer. Yet as he writes to Timothy (2 Timothy 4:20) when his friend, Trophimus, was ill, Paul was forced to leave Trophimus at Miletus. Evidently Paul was unable to call upon God's healing power to cure him.

So Paul also saw the need for action. He had his own personal physician in his friend Luke. He evidently assumed that God was at work in the skills of his "beloved physician." He made plans to take action, as he did when he told the Roman church that he would move on to Spain after visiting them (Romans 15:24).

When to Pray and When to Act

How do we handle this business of prayer versus action? I don't suppose it has been summed up any better than the old saying, "Work like it was all up to you, and pray as though it was all up to God."

Let's draw an illustration from the Old Testament. When Nehemiah returned to the destroyed Jerusalem, he carefully surveyed the work that needed to be done (Nehemiah 2:11-16). Next, he organized the people to build the wall. But while all this was going on, Sanballat and the enemies of the Jews plotted together to come and fight against Jerusalem and cause confusion (Nehemiah 4:9, RSV). Nehemiah's response to this was classic: "And we prayed to our God, and set a guard as a protection against them day and night."

Nehemiah did both; he worked and he prayed. And while they were building, they were always ready for the enemy: "Those who carried burdens were laden in such a way that each with one hand labored on the work and with the other held his weapon. And each of the builders had a sword girded at his side while he built" (Nehemiah 4:17, 18, RSV).

We, too, are told to be girded with a sword: "And take the helmet of salvation, and the sword of the Spirit, which is the word of God. Pray at all times in the Spirit, with all prayer and supplication" (Ephesians 6:17, 18a, RSV).

But some will answer, "Look, I *have* prayed. And God didn't answer my prayer as He promised!"

Must God Answer—Always?

Must God always answer prayer?

Or perhaps to put it another way, must God always answer prayer the way we would like Him to? Ah, the paradox again. J. B. Phillips in his delightful book *Your God Is Too Small* speaks of "God in a box." How neatly we sometimes put Him there to do our bidding.

We, as men and women, dare to question God!

My former pastor, Ray Ortlund, said one time that in the Bible, "God has stooped to talk mantalk." Friends, the God of the universe stoops to answer man's prayer. God stands outside His created system. He has no need to conform to that which He has created. When we as the creature demand that the Creator be part of His own system, He is no longer God.

But we are part of God's system. We live with one foot in the kingdom and one foot in this life.

Pray as though it was entirely up to God. Work as though it was entirely up to you.

Again the tension. If we let our faith hinge on the "responses" to our prayers, we stand in constant peril of having it completely shattered.

If we leave God out of our living, if we see Him as disinterested in our everyday life, we are people of no-faith.

"Oh, that's too hard!" you reply.

Yes, it's hard. But not *too* hard. It's the way God is.

Notes

1. The interpretation of this particular passage in James is ambiguous. The usage of the Greek words for both "sick" and "save" is such that either a completely spiritual or a completely physical interpretation could be given. It can be interpreted to mean that the person will be ultimately saved in the resurrection or that he will be saved from no infirmity. Some have suggested that James purposely left the ambiguity, that both ideas are considered.

Notice the larger context. The discussion on healing is seen as one of our possible responses to the world around. If we are cheerful, let us sing praises (to God) for that which makes us cheerful. If we are suffering, let us pray to the same God. If we are sick to the point where for some reason we are unable to help ourselves by direct intercession or other means, call for the representatives of Christ's church.

2. I like the title of Richard Foster's excellent book on the spiritual life: *Celebration of Discipline*.

19
DEPENDENCE VERSUS INDEPENDENCE

My brothers, if any of you should wander away from the truth and another should turn him back on to the right path, then the latter may be sure that in turning a man back from his wandering course he has rescued a soul from death, and in so doing will "cover a multitude of sins" (James 5:19, 20).

It seems quite fitting that we should end on a note of our dependence upon one another and the tension this causes among people who very much like to be independent. Christians are people who have found a new relationship; not only a vertical relationship with the Lord of the universe, but a new interdependent relationship on a horizontal level. We are stuck with each other.

The psychologist Erik Erikson notes that human beings go through three stages in their development. In the beginning, at the time of their birth, they are completely *dependent* upon others. Everything they do, their complete life, is in the hands of someone else. But as they grow older, as they approach the teenage years, they go through a process of *independence*. We talk about young people "rebelling." But this seems to be a necessary part of the process of maturation. Erikson points out that it's only after people have gone through this period of independence that they can become *interdependent*. If they stay at the point of independence, they will be very lonely people, they will never really mature.[1]

How similar that is to the Christian life. Too often we find Christians who have become stunted in their growth because they never learned that they were part of a body. They never learned about the give and take of interdependence.

The Difficulty with Interdependence

It is difficult to be interdependent. It is much easier to adopt the one role as given or received and stick to it. Bishop Stephen Neill has pointed out that the game of life is always played out between the poles. The moment we cluster around one end of the field and become polarized, then we are no longer playing the game.

It is this interdependence that keeps us whole, that helps us to stay clear of sin, to stay in the center of the pathway of truth. It is when we become independent and go our own way that we are most likely to be in danger. This is the place that James finds us as we conclude our study of his letters (James 5:19-20, RSV).

"My brethren, if any among you . . ."[2]

James is speaking to those who know Christ.

". . . wanders from the truth . . ."

Whether we are speaking of the Christian or the seeker among the body of Christians, we can understand what it means to wander from the truth. "The truth shall make you free" (John 8:32, KJV). To know the truth is to be free. To wander from the truth is to be in bondage.

The path of goodness and righteousness lies before us. It is an all too familiar road. Most of us know very well what we should do. But off to the side of this well-worn path is a lovely patch of spring flowers or perhaps a curious rock formation. How interesting it looks! We wander a bit from the path to see what it is or observe it more closely. We'll only be gone from the path for a moment. But at once our attention is captured by yet another more lovely scene, and we move further away to enjoy it.

Before we realize what has happened, we can't find our way back to the path. Perhaps we don't want to, we don't even care. Perhaps we have become engrossed with new vistas. We may not even be aware that we couldn't get back to the path by ourselves if we wanted to. We are "lost," and we don't even know it. We need a rescue party.

Who Should Be the Rescuer?

". . . some one brings him back . . ."

Here's where the rub comes. Who is that "some one?" Who's the person most skilled to go and find us? Who is most qualified? Who decides we are lost in the first place and takes the responsibility to organize the search and rescue team?

There are a few things to keep in mind here.

1. If we are not part of a concerned group, if our life is not woven into the fabric of the local church, chances are that no one will ever know we are lost.[3] Sometimes people leave a local church in disagreement with what's going on. But even though they disagree and have left, they more or less expect (hope) that someone will come looking for them, someone will make that phone call to ask why they haven't been around. When weeks go by and they haven't heard, they become bitter and complaining. Yet they never had anything to complain about. For they never gave up part of their independence to become part of a group.

2. Putting the shoe on the other foot, there is a responsibility of all the members to make sure that each brother and sister "fits in." It is much like a company that hires a new employee. The company knows much more about the total situation than the person joining them. Consequently, they have a responsibility to "make her succeed." This takes work, often hard work. It means that we have to learn to know each other, and some of us are difficult to know!

One would never think of inviting someone home for an evening and then paying no attention to them, spending no thought on what they would like to do or their interest. How strange that we invite people to join our local fellowship and expect them immediately to assume the responsibility for feeling at home.

Part of this fitting in is to make sure that people understand the *goals* of the local fellowship, even as they are incorporated into it. The reason a good many Christians "go out the back door" of the church is they discovered once they had entered the fellowship that it was not what they expected when they came. They just didn't agree with what they perceived to be its goals.[4]

3. But assuming that we are in fellowship with believers, to what extent should others go in turning us back if we wander from the church?

The biblical concept is not one of watchful waiting to see who steps out of line or is straying. This immediately makes us into judges, evaluators of each other's actions. Rather, we need active participation with one another that will keep each other's attention on Christ and His body: stirring one another up to love and good works (Hebrews 9:24), breaking bread together and praying (Acts 2:42), weeping with those who weep and rejoicing with those who rejoice (1 Corinthians 12:26), being concerned about the other person's business (Philippians 2:4).

These are the things that will immediately indicate who should do the rescuing.

Turning Our Lives Over to Others

In our Pathfinder Sunday school class, the majority of the people were in small groups of one type or another. It was exciting to see what a difference these groups can make when one of their members encounters marital difficulty or spiritual weariness. They know who is responsible to care for these people

". . . let him know . . ."

This is a worthy occupation, this bringing back a sinner. Should we be confrontive or reflective? Should we admonish or admit our own failure? Again the passage from Galatians 6:1, 2 (NIV)—that, too, is good advice: "Brothers, if someone is caught in a sin, you who are spiritual should restore him gently. But watch yourself, or you also may be tempted. Carry each other's burdens, and in this way you will fulfill the law of Christ."

Be prepared to be confrontive. To be prepared to admonish another means that we have shown a willingness to be admonished *ourselves*, that we have shown a willingness to confess our own sin. How easy it is for me to tell other people what they should do! How hard it is for me to accept that same advice! So let us confess our own sins as we discover them (James 5:16), so that the other person can see *his* own need and realize that we come to him not from a superior position, but that we too know what it means to wander from the path.

". . . save his soul from death . . ."

"The soul that sins shall die." Separation from God is death. Perhaps we don't fully comprehend the horror of death until we face this fact of separation. Paul told his Athenian audience, "In him we live and move and have our being" (Acts 17:28, RSV). When we are separated from Him, we no longer have our being. We are lost. We are dead.

"... will cover a multitude of sins."

Obviously not the sins of "some one" bringing the person back, but the sins of that person who has wandered and has come back. Perhaps the key to *why* these sins will be covered is found in the similar use of the same idiom by Peter: "Above all, love each other deeply, because love covers a multitude of sins" (1 Peter 4:8, NIV).

That's what the gospel is all about, isn't it? And if we as part of Christ's body extend His love to others, should we be surprised that this love will in some way manage to be the cleanser that will make that person fresh and clean again? "You see, at just the right time, when we were still powerless, Christ died for the ungodly. But God demonstrates his own love for us in this: While we were still sinners, Christ died for us" (Romans 5:6, 8, NIV).

To be interdependent is to be in tension. It is a difficult thing to continuously turn over our lives to one another. But again the paradox: the more we give ourselves away, the more whole we become.

> As each has received a gift, employ it for one another, as good stewards of God's varied grace (1 Peter 4:10, RSV).

Notes

1. Erik Erikson, *Identity: Youth and Crisis.*

2. This difficult section, rendered here in the Revised Standard Version, is the pivot on which the interpretation of the rest of the passage hinges. "Among you" may mean those who are already Christians, or it could mean those who had not yet found the light of Christ, but were among this body of believers as seekers. The writer to the Hebrews gives us hints that it is possible to have once been enlightened, to have tasted the heavenly gift, become partakers of the Holy Spirit, and still commit apostasy such that it is impossible to restore them (Hebrews 6:4-6). But this would appear to contradict James's view that someone can restore them.

Perhaps, as is so often the case with James, it is best to take a middle view. Only God knows when a man is truly born into the kingdom, when he becomes sealed with the mark of the Holy Spirit. There may be those who walk among us who appear to have all the marks of a Christian and yet still have not made that final surrender to the Liberator.

3. If we take the view that the one who has wandered never really knew Christ, then we see the dramatic need for the new Christian to be immediately made a working part of the body, however weak they may be. This business of putting new Christians in positions of responsibility within

the body is no easy task, but it's one that we have to wrestle with within our Western society and in our overseas missions.

4. See Lyle Schaller, *The Change Agent*. In Part II of *Whatever Happened to Commitment?* I have tried to deal with this process of getting into a local fellowship. For some help in building an accountability group, see Louis Evans, Jr., *Covenant to Care*.

20
POSTSCRIPT

We live in a day in which everyone wants answers. We want to know. We want to be in control. What the Bible tells us is the Christian is the one who has turned the control center of his life over to Christ.

Now this does not mean that we no longer ask questions, or that we refuse to use our intellect. There is an intimate connection between giving ourselves to Christ and intellectually grasping what this means: "Therefore, I urge you, brothers, in view of God's mercy, to offer your bodies as living sacrifices, holy and pleasing to God—which is your spiritual worship. Do not conform any longer to the pattern of this world, but be transformed *by the renewing of your mind*. Then you will be able to test and approve what God's will is—his good, pleasing and perfect will" (Romans 12:1, 2, NIV).

Use your mind. Use it to understand that God will be God. His ways are not our ways. The moment that we have all the "answers," we will no longer need God. We will have rationalized Him completely away.

Every corner newsstand holds another how-to-do-it book. It seems that a new seminar about some aspect of the Christian life is planned every day. These are good and helpful in themselves, but their goodness lies not in the answers they give; their goodness comes from the new understanding that they give us of God's Word, how we can live in light of it.

POSTSCRIPT

Because God's ways are not our ways, the Bible is a book of paradox, of seeming contradictions as far as man is concerned, but God's good and best for us as far as He is concerned.

These paradoxes call us to live in tension, to live life out between the polarities to which we are so easily attracted. The answer to living in tension is to live in faith. God is the one who is *for* us.

Live in paradox! Live in tension! Live in the faith that ours is a God who is for us! Live in the faith that goes further.

In the midst of joy and anguish and hope and despair, live *life!* Not as men and women who do not know the meaning and purpose of life, but as those who do.

BIBLIOGRAPHY

Augustine, Saint. *City of God*. New York: Doubleday and Co., Inc., 1957.

Barnet, Richard J. *The Lean Years: Politics in the Age of Scarcity*. New York: Simon & Schuster, 1980.

Barnet, Richard J. and Ronald E. Muller. *Global Reach: The Power of the Multinational Corporation*. New York: Simon & Schuster, 1974.

Becker, Ernest. *Denial of Death*. New York: Free Press, 1983.

Bell, Daniel. *The Cultural Contradictions of Capitalism*. New York: Basic Books, Inc., 1976.

Berger, Peter L. *Facing Up to Modernity: Excursions in Sociology, Politics and Religion*. New York: Basic Books, Inc., 1979.

_____ . *Pyramids of Sacrifice: Political Ethics and Social Change*. New York: Doubleday, 1976.

Berger, Peter L., et al. *The Homeless Mind*. New York: Vintage Books, 1973.

Berger, Peter L. and Richard J. Neuhaus. *Against the World for the World*. New York: The Seabury Press, 1976.

Berne, Eric. *The Games People Play*. New York: Ballatine Books, 1978.

Bloesch, Donald G. *The Evangelical Renaissance*. Grand Rapids, Mich.: William B. Eerdmans, 1973.

Bonhoeffer, Dietrich. *The Cost of Discipleship*. New York: Macmillan Publishing Company, 1967.

_____ . *Letters and Papers from Prison*. New York: Macmillan Publishing Company, 1953.

Brandt, Willy and Anthony Sampson, eds. *North-South: A Program for Survival*. Cambridge: MIT Press, 1980.

Bright, John. *The Kingdom of God*. Nashville: Abingdon Press, 1953.

Churchman, C. West. *The Systems Approach*. New York: Dell Publishing Company, 1968.

Costas, Orlando E. *The Church and Its Mission: A Shattering Critique from the Third World*. Wheaton: Tyndale House, 1975.

Dayton, Donald W. *Discovering an Evangelical Heritage*. New York: Harper and Row, 1976.

Dayton, Edward R. *God's Purpose/Man's Plans*. Monrovia, Calif.: MARC, 1971.

BIBLIOGRAPHY

_____. *That Everyone May Hear*. Monrovia, Calif.: MARC, 1979, 1981, 1983.

_____. *Tools for Time Management*. Grand Rapids, Mich.: Zondervan, 1974.

_____. *Whatever Happened to Commitment?* Grand Rapids, Mich.: Zondervan, 1984.

Dayton, Edward R. and Ted W. Engstrom. *Strategy for Living: How to Make the Best Use of Your Time and Abilities*. Glendale, Calif.: Regal Books, 1976.

_____. *Strategy for Leadership*. Old Tappan, N.J.: Fleming H. Revell, Co., 1978.

Dayton, Edward R. and David A. Fraser. *Planning Strategies for World Evangelization*. Grand Rapids, Mich.: William B. Eerdmans, 1979.

Dayton, Edward R. and Samuel Wilson. *Unreached Peoples '82*. Monrovia, Calif.: MARC, 1982.

Dennis, Lane. *A Reason for Hope*. Old Tappan, N.J.: Fleming H. Revell, Co., 1976.

De Toqueville, Alexis. *Democracy in America*. Edited by Richard O. Heffner. New York: The New American Library, 1956.

Dobson, James. *Hide or Seek*. Old Tappan, N.J.: Fleming H. Revell, Co., 1974.

Drakeford, John. *The Awesome Power of the Listening Ear*. Waco, Tex.: Word Books, 1967.

Drucker, Peter. *Adventures of a Bystander*. New York: Harper and Row, 1980.

Erikson, Erik. *Identity: Youth and Crisis*. New York: W. W. Norton and Co., 1968.

Evans, Louis H., Jr. *Covenant to Care*. Wheaton, Ill: Victor Books, 1982.

Ferguson, Marilyn. *The Aquarian Conspiracy: Personal and Social Transformation in the 1980s*. Los Angeles: J. P. Taveher, 1981.

Ferré, Nels. *The Extreme Center*. Waco, Tex.: Word Books, 1973.

Fitzgerald, Francis. *America Revised*. Boston: Little, Brown and Company, 1979.

Florovsky, Georges. *Christianity and Culture*. Belmont: Nordland Publishing Company, 1974.

Foster, George M. *Traditional Cultures and the Impact of Technological Change*. New York: Harper and Row, 1962.

Foster, Richard J. *Celebration of Discipline: Paths to Spiritual Growth*. New York: Harper and Row, 1978.

Freire, Paulo. *Pedagogy of the Oppressed*. New York: The Seabury Press, 1970.

Friesen, Garry and J. Robin Maxson. *Decision Making and the Will of God*. Portland, Ore.: Multnomah Press, 1980.

Gaebelein, Frank E. *The Practical Epistle of James*. Great Neck, N.Y.: Donigen and Raughley, 1955.

Gallup, George, Jr., and David Poling. *The Search for America's Faith*. Nashville: Abingdon, 1980.

Gardner, John W. *Excellence: Can We Be Equal and Excellent Too?* New York: Harper and Row, 1971.

Getz, Gene A. *Sharpening the Focus of the Church*. Chicago: Moody Press, 1976.

Goodwin, Richard. *The American Condition*. New York: Doubleday and Company, 1974.

Greeley, Andrew M. *Why Can't They Be Like Us? America's White Ethnic Groups*. New York: E. P. Dutton & Company, 1971.

Green, Michael. *Evangelism in the Early Church*. Grand Rapids, Mich.: William B. Eerdmans Publishing Co., 1970.

Gross, Martin. *The Psychological Society*. New York: Random House, 1978.

Halberstam, David. *The Best and the Brightest*. New York: Random House, 1972.

Hall, Brian P. *Value Clarifications As Learning Process: A Guidebook for Educators*. New York: Paulist Press, 1974.

Harper, Michael. *A New Way of Living*. Plainfield, N.J.: Logos, 1973.

Harrington, Michael. *The Other America: Poverty in the United States*. Baltimore: Penguin Books, 1963.

Hatfield, Mark. *Between a Rock and a Hard Place*. Waco, Tex.: Word Books, 1976.

Heilbroner, Robert L. and Aaron Singer. *The Economic Transformation of America*. New York: Harcourt, Brace, Jovanovich, 1977.

Henderson, Hazel. *Creating Alternative Futures*. New York: Perigee, 1978.

Henry, Carl F. H. *Evangelicals in Search of Identity*. Waco: Word Books, 1976.

Herzberg, Frederick. *Work and the Nature of Man*. New York: T. Y. Crowell, 1966.

Johnson, Warren. *Muddling Toward Frugality*. Niwot, Colo.: Sierra Publications, 1978.

Jones, E. Stanley. *The Unshakable Kingdom and the Unchanging Person*. New York: Abingdon Press, 1972.

Kahn, Herman. *World Economic Development*. Boulder, Colo.: Westview Press, 1979.

Kenniston, Kenneth and the Carnegie Council on Children. *All Our Children*. New York: Harcourt, Brace, Jovanovich, 1977.

Kennedy, Gerald. *The Lion and the Lamb: Paradoxes of the Christian Faith*. New York: Abingdon Press, 1950.

Kennedy, James D. *Evangelism Explosion*. Wheaton, Ill.: Tyndale, 1970.

BIBLIOGRAPHY

Kiev, Ari. *A Strategy for Daily Living*. New York: Free Press, 1973.

Kraus, C. Norman. *The Community of the Spirit*. Grand Rapids, Mich.: William B. Eerdmans Publishing Co., 1973.

Kraybill, Donald B. *The Upside Down Kingdom*. Scottsdale, Pa.: Herald Press, 1978.

Ladd, George E. *The Gospel of the Kingdom*. Grand Rapids, Mich.: William B. Eerdmans Publishing Company, 1959.

Lasch, Christopher. *The Culture of Narcissism: American Life in an Age of Diminishing Expectations*. New York: W. W. Norton and Co., Inc., 1979.

Ledered, William J. and Eugene Burdick. *The Ugly American*. New York: W. W. Norton and Co., Inc., 1958.

Levinson, Harry. *The Exceptional Executive*. Cambridge, Mass.: Harvard University Press, 1968.

Lindsell, Harold. *Battle for the Bible*. Grand Rapids, Mich.: Zondervan, 1978.

Marsden, George M. *Fundamentalism and American Culture*. New York: Oxford University Press, 1980.

Marty, Martin E. *A Nation of Behaviors*. Chicago: University of Chicago Press, 1976.

Maslow, Abraham H. *Motivation and Personality*. New York: Harper and Row, 1970.

McGregor, Douglas. *The Human Side of Organization*. New York: McGraw-Hill, 1960.

_____. *Professional Manager*. New York: McGraw-Hill, 1967.

Mellis, Charles J. *Committed Communities: Fresh Streams for World Missions*. Pasadena, Calif.: William Carey Library, 1976.

Menninger, Karl. *Whatever Became of Sin?* New York: Bantam Books, 1978.

Mollenkott, Virginia. *In Search of Balance*. Waco, Tex.: Word Books, 1969.

Mooneyham, W. Stanley. *What Do You Say to a Hungry World?* Waco, Tex.: Word Books, 1975.

Mouw, Richard. *Called to Holy Worldliness*. Philadelphia: Fortress Press, 1980.

Mowrer, O. Hobart. *The New Group Therapy*. New York: Van Nostrand Company, 1964.

Niebuhr, H. Richard. *Christ and Culture*. New York: Harper and Row, 1951.

Novak, Michael. *The Rise of the Unmeltable Ethnics*, New York: Macmillan, 1972.

O'Connor, Elizabeth. *The Eighth Day of Creation*. Waco, Tex.: Word Books, 1971.

_____. *Journey Inward, Journey Outward*. New York: Harper & Row, 1975.

_____. *The New Community*. New York: Harper and Row, 1976.

Ortlund, Raymond C. *Lord, Make My Life a Miracle*. Glendale, Calif.: Regal Books, 1974.

Phillips, J. B. *Your God Is Too Small*. New York: Macmillan Publishing Company, Inc., 1953.

_____. *The New Testament in Modern English*. New York: Macmillan Publishing Company, Inc., 1958.

Quebedeaux, Richard. *The Worldly Evangelicals*. New York: Harper and Row, 1978.

_____. *By What Authority*. New York: Harper and Row, 1982.

Ramm, Bernard L. *The Right, the Good, and the Happy*. Waco, Tex.: Word Books, 1971.

Rifkin, Jeremy and Ted Howard. *The Emerging Order: God in the Age of Scarcity*. New York: Putnam, 1979.

Rogers, Jack. *Biblical Authority*. Waco, Tex.: Word Books, 1977.

Rose, Stephen C. *The Grass Roots Church*. New York: Holt, Rinehart and Winston, 1966.

Schaller, Lyle. *The Change Agent: The Strategy of Innovative Leadership*. Nashville: Abingdon, 1972.

Schumacher, E. F. *A Guide for the Perplexed*. New York: Harper and Row, 1977.

_____. *Small Is Beautiful: Economics as if People Mattered*. New York: Harper and Row, 1975.

Schur, Edwin M. *Awareness Trap: Self Absorption Instead of Social Change*. New York: McGraw-Hill, 1977.

Sennett, Richard. *Fall of Public Man: The Social Psychology of Capitalism*. New York: Random House, 1978.

Selye, Hans. *Stress Without Distress*. New York: Signet, 1974.

Sheehy, Gail. *Passages*. New York: E. P. Dutton, 1974.

_____. *Pathfinders*. New York: William Morrow, 1981.

Sider, Ronald J. *Rich Christians in an Age of Hunger: A Biblical Study*. Downers Grove: InterVarsity Press, 1977.

Skinner, B. F. *Beyond Freedom and Dignity*. New York: Bantam Books, 1971.

Smart, James D. *The Cultural Subversion of the Biblical Faith*. Philadelphia: Westminster Press, 1977.

Snyder, Howard A. *The Community of the King*. Downers Grove: InterVarsity Press, 1977.

Stewart, Edward C. *American Cultural Patterns: A Cross-Cultural Perspective*. Chicago: Intercultural Press, 1971.

Taylor, John V. *Enough Is Enough: A Biblical Call for Moderation in a Consumer Oriented Society*. Minneapolis: Augsburg Publishing House, 1977.

125

BIBLIOGRAPHY

Trueblood, Elton. *Company of the Committed*. New York: Harper and Row, 1961.

Vanier, Jean. *Community and Growth*. New York: Paulist Press, 1979.

Wagner, C. Peter. *Your Spiritual Gifts Can Help Your Church Grow*. Glendale, Calif.: Regal Books, 1979.

_____ . *Our Kind of People*. Atlanta: John Knox Press, 1979.

Wagner, C. Peter and Edward R. Dayton. *Unreached Peoples 79, 80, 81*. Elgin, Ill.: David C. Cook, 1979, 1980, 1981.

Wallis, Jim. *An Agenda for Biblical People*. New York: Harper and Row, 1976.

_____ . *The Call to Conversion*. New York: Harper and Row, 1981.

Webber, Robert. *Common Roots: A Call to Evangelical Maturity*. Grand Rapids, Mich.: Zondervan, 1978.

_____ . *The Secular Saint: A Case for Evangelical Social Responsibility*. Grand Rapids, Mich.: Zondervan, 1979.

Webber, Robert and Donald Bloesch. *The Orthodox Evangelicals*. New York: Thomas Nelson, 1978.

Weber, Max. *The Protestant Ethic and the Spirit of Capitalism*. New York: Scribner, 1977.

Yankelovich, Daniel. *New Rules: Searching for Self-Fulfillment in a World Turned Upside Down*. New York: Random House, 1981.

Yoder, John G. *The Politics of Jesus*. Grand Rapids, Mich.: William B. Eerdmans Publishing Company, 1972.

Scripture Index

Subject Index

SUBJECT INDEX